Jonah

and the Meaning of Our Lives

A VERSE-BY-VERSE
CONTEMPORARY
COMMENTARY

Rabbi Steven Bob

The Jewish Publication Society | Philadelphia

Library of Congress Cataloging-in-Publication Data
Names: Bob, Steven M., 1950–, author.
Title: Jonah and the meaning of our lives: a verse-by-verse contemporary commentary / Rabbi Steven Bob.
Description: Philadelphia: Jewish Publication Society; Lincoln: University of Nebraska Press, [2016] | 2016
Identifiers: LCCN 2016003065 (print)
LCCN 2016003462 (ebook)
ISBN 9780827612204 (pbk.: alk. paper)
ISBN 9780827612839 (epub)
ISBN 9780827612846 (mobi)
ISBN 9780827612853 (pdf)
Subjects: LCSH: Bible. Jonah—Criticism, interpretation, etc.
Classification: LCC BS1605.52 .B63 2016 (print) | LCC BS1605.52 (ebook) | DDC 224/.92077—dc23
LC record available at http://lccn .loc.gov/2016003065

Set in Scala by Rachel Gould.

Jeffery & Deb

I hope that you enjoy these stories about Jonah

[signature]

Jonah *and the Meaning of Our Lives*

University of Nebraska Press | Lincoln

I dedicate this book to my partner
in all things for over forty years,
my ezer k'negdo: my wife, Tammie

Contents

Preface

When I was a child, I heard the story of Jonah as a story about God. It was presented to me as an entertaining tale teaching that God's power extends to all corners of the earth. I now see it as a story about Jonah. As an adult I am drawn to this story because I feel that I know Jonah. He is not a heroic knight of faith like Abraham. When God calls Abraham to offer his son Isaac as a sacrifice, Abraham gets up early in the morning and goes, but when God calls Jonah, Jonah runs away. I don't know anybody who is like Abraham. I know lots of people who are like Jonah.

I am drawn to the book of Jonah not only because I know many like him but also because Jonah receives a second chance. After God caused the fish to spew Jonah back onto dry land, God could have said to him, "I forgive you for fleeing. Now go home. I will send another, more dependable prophet to Nineveh. Perhaps Elijah is available for this mission." But God doesn't dismiss Jonah; God gives him another opportunity. This is deep forgiveness, forgiveness with renewed trust. God fully accepts Jonah's repentance. God sees Jonah as fit for the mission of carrying the Divine word to Nineveh.

We always want a second chance. We'd like everybody we have wronged to give *us* another opportunity, but are we willing to give *others* a second chance? Not simply forgiving the people who wronged us, but trusting them again in circumstances in which they had previously disappointed us. This is a serious challenge. Will we trust the person who mismanaged the money to handle the finances again? Will we trust the person who was less than loyal to be our friend again? The situations occur in each of our lives, at work, with our friends and our families. God's full forgiveness of Jonah is a model for us.

Humor plays a key role in my life, and I'm pleased to see exaggeration and humor in the story of Jonah: the size of Nineveh, the extent of the repentance of the Ninevites, the animals of Nineveh putting on sackcloth, the storm, and Jonah in the belly of the big fish. The humor draws us into the story. And if we look more closely, we will find profound lessons that can help us understand our lives. I hope that this book will provide an opportunity for you to look at challenges you face from new perspectives and examine the meaning of your life as you reflect upon the meaning of Jonah and his story.

Acknowledgments

Many people have assisted me in the journey toward the completion of this book. I appreciate their encouragement, support, and specific suggestions.

This entire project grew out of a conversation with Rabbi Barry Schwartz, director of the Jewish Publication Society. When I inquired about the possibility of JPS publishing my translation of the commentaries to Jonah, he asked me, how does one teach Jonah? He then suggested that I follow that model in creating this book. I am grateful for his vision and for his confidence in me. Carol Hupping, the managing editor of JPS, worked closely with me to improve my text. She helped me focus the content of the book and raise the level of the prose. I am grateful to Elaine Durham Otto for copyediting the text and to my project manager at the University of Nebraska Press, Ann Baker.

My friends Rabbi Norman Cohen, Rabbi Mark Dov Shapiro, Rabbi Charles Levi, Rabbi Elliot Strom, Rabbi Howard Sommer, Jody Weinberg, and Rabbi Michael Weinberg each read a portion of my manuscript and provided support through years of friendship.

The leaders and members of Congregation Etz Chaim give me a monthlong study leave every January. They understand that in order to teach new and engaging texts, I must continue to learn.

The participants in my Jonah study group at Etz Chaim enthusiastically gathered every Friday at noon for two years to study the book of Jonah verse by verse.

The teens of the Chalutzim program at Olin Sang Ruby Union Institute who have been part of my Jonah and the Meaning of Life class over the years sharpened my thinking with their questions and comments.

My wife, Tammie, has been my partner in all things. She carefully read the entire manuscript. She helped bring clarity and style to its language and content. Her comments and suggestions keep me balanced.

Introduction

In Pirke Avot 5:26 Ben Bag Bag famously teaches, "Turn it, turn it, for it contains everything. Look into it, grow old and worn over it, and never move away from it, for you will find no better portion than it." While most people take these words to describe the Torah, for me they describe the book of Jonah. In this short book of the Bible, we can find answers to the most important questions that people ask: Who am I? Why am I here? What provides meaning to my life?

This book is a journey through the Jonah story, verse by verse, with some of the great Bible commentators—Rashi, Abraham Ibn Ezra, David Kimchi, Isaac Abarbanel, and the Malbim—other biblical and rabbinic sources, and my own comments, drawn from personal anecdotes, literature, history, and popular culture. If you are unfamiliar with the commentators I cite, let me introduce you to them.

The Commentators

RASHI

Rabbi Shlomo Yitzhaki (1040–1105) is better known by the acronym Rashi. He spent most of his life in Troyes, in the Champagne area of northern France. He studied in Worms in the yeshiva of Rabbi Yaakov ben Yakar, and then in Mainz with Rabbi Yitzhak ben Yehudah. He returned to Troyes, where he established his own yeshiva. Rashi wrote a commentary on the entire Hebrew Bible and on the entire Talmud. For most scholars, completing either one of these projects would be considered a life's work. In addition to his scholarship, Rashi earned his living as a wine merchant.

Rashi's commentary to the Hebrew Bible provides the foundation for ongoing conversation about its meaning. Rashi's commentary on Jonah is much shorter than the later commentaries; he does not comment on each verse and does not launch into long theological arguments, as later commentators do.

In his commentary on Jonah, Rashi draws upon chapter 10 of Pirke de Rabbi Eliezer, a ninth-century collection of midrash. He often refers to the Targum, a translation of the Bible into Aramaic, the everyday spoken language of the rabbinic period. And so the Aramaic translation is helpful to Rashi in clarifying the meaning of difficult phrases, and he shares with his readers how the author of the Targum understood the word. The Talmudic tradition attributes the authorship of the Targum to the books of the prophets to Jonathan ben Uzziel. It is therefore called Targum Yonaton.

ABRAHAM IBN EZRA

Abrahami Ibn Ezra's life (ca. 1092–1167) bridged the Muslim and Christian worlds. He was born in Muslim Spain and moved to Christian Italy in the middle of his life, fleeing the fundamentalist Almohades dynasty. He brought learning previously published in Arabic to the Christian world. In his commentary he draws on the Geonim and others who lived in the Arabic-speaking lands.

In addition to his commentary on the books of the Hebrew Bible, Ibn Ezra wrote about Hebrew grammar, philosophy, astronomy, and poetry. He is rigorous in his analysis, making use of a careful reading of the grammar of individual words. He avoids fanciful midrashic interpretation, and his comments are often terse. He expects much from his readers. Of all the commentators contained in this volume, he requires the most explanation. In his brief comments Ibn Ezra often presents important theological ideas.

RABBI DAVID KIMCHI

Rabbi David Kimchi (1160–1235) is known by the Hebrew acronym RaDaK. He was born in Narbonne, which is in the southeastern corner of what is now France. During Kimchi's life the Catalan dynasty of Barcelona ruled this area, called Provence. The Kimchi family came to Christian Narbonne from the Muslim-controlled portion of Spain, fleeing the fundamentalist Almohades dynasty.

David Kimchi was part of a scholarly family. His father, Rabbi

Joseph Kimchi, and his brother, Rabbi Moses Kimchi, were both noted Bible commentators. He quotes his father in his commentary to the book of Jonah. David Kimchi was an important scholar of Hebrew grammar and wrote *Michlol*, an early comprehensive study of it.

One could describe Kimchi's commentary as psychological. He examines Jonah's inner process, telling us what Jonah must have been thinking as events in his story unfolded, using what might be described as Jonah's "voice-over." We will see this particularly as Jonah prays from the belly of the big fish.

In Pirke Avot 3:17 Rabbi Eliezer ben Azariah teaches, "Ein Kemach Ein Torah—where there is no flour there is no Torah," meaning when people do not have food to eat they cannot study. Kimchi's students adapted this text to say, "Ein Kimchi Ein Torah—when there is no Kimchi there is no Torah."

DON ISAAC ABARBANEL

Isaac Abarbanel (1437–1508) was a financier, an advisor to royalty, a philosopher, and a Bible commentator. He was a prominent leader of the Jewish community of Portugal and Spain during the difficult times of the expulsion of the Jews from those countries.

His approach differs from the earlier commentators in content, structure, and style. He does not delve into the grammar issues explored by Ibn Ezra and Kimchi, but rather focuses on the narrative line of the text.

Abarbanel explains his ideas fully. He does not depend on his readers to bring as much background or to read as "actively" as do the earlier commentators. He writes in long, complex sentences and draws on rabbinic sources. He refers to *Seder Olam*, an early rabbinic chronology, and quotes from Pirke de Rabbi Eliezer. He refers to Abraham Ibn Ezra as "My Teacher," whether he is agreeing or disagreeing with him and also cites David Kimchi's commentary.

MALBIM

Meir Leibush ben Yechiel Michel (1809–79), widely known as the

Malbim, lived in Eastern and Central Europe. He was a staunch defender of traditional Judaism in the modern age, often clashing with community leaders who wished to modernize Jewish worship and religious life. Born in Volochisk, Russia, and educated in Warsaw, he was rabbi in Wreschen (Prussia), Kempen (Prussia), Kherson (Ukraine), and Moghilev (Belarus). His most prominent position was as chief rabbi of Bucharest.

Between 1845 and 1870, the Malbim wrote a commentary on the entire Hebrew Bible, the first such effort to do so since the Middle Ages. In his commentary on the book of Jonah we will see his resistance to modernist tendencies. The Malbim takes the midrash seriously.

Note to Readers

All of the translations of the Bible commentators in this volume are mine. At times the commentators assume that their readers have more knowledge of traditional Jewish sources than we do, and so I occasionally add words in brackets to fill in the gaps in their comments.

The biblical quotations follow the New Jewish Publication Society (NJPS) translation, except when the commentators' remarks only make sense if we begin with a more literal translation of a word or two. I also translate the four-letter name of God as the Eternal, a gender-neutral term, rather than the masculine term, Lord, found in the NJPS. When the original Hebrew text of Jonah refers to the Deity as Elohim, I follow the NJPS translation, God.

The commentators also use the four-letter name and Elohim, as well as various other names for the Deity, and I translate these in ways that I think best convey the commentators' original expressions of God the Blessed One, the Holy One of Blessing, God, Who Is Blessed, the One God, and the God of Heaven. When they use Hashem, literally "the Name," I maintain Hashem in my transliteration of their comments. The quotations from the Christian Scripture follow NSRV translation.

Jonah *and the Meaning of Our Lives*

~~~~~~

Our Names and Identities

Who Are We?

And the word of the Eternal came to Jonah son of Amittai. —JONAH 1:1

The most basic question a person can ask us is "Who are you?" In response we might identify ourselves by profession, family ties, accomplishments, location, lineage, and affiliations. But our first response generally is to introduce ourselves with our name.

According to a midrash, "There are three names by which a person is called: one that his father and mother call him, one that other people call him, and one that he earns for himself. The best of all is the one that he earns for himself" (*Tanhuma*, Parshat *Vayak'hel*).

I am Steve Bob. My mother calls me Steven. My congregants call me Rabbi Bob. Three people call me Dad. To seven people I am Grandpa. Many of my friends call me Simcha.

Simcha is my given Hebrew name, after my mother's father. Simcha means joy, and it is a perfect name for me. I am as positive and happy a person as exists. Simcha is the name my parents gave me, and it is a name I earn every day. A famous phrase applies to me: "He is just like his name (*kain k'mo shmo hu*)."

This phrase comes from the Bible. Nabal's wife, Abigail, explains his character to King David: "He is just what his name says" (1 Samuel 25:25).

In the Bible, as in other literature, the characters' names often tell us a lot about them. The main character in our story also resembles his name.

Jonah in the original Hebrew is Yonah. A person who does not know Hebrew will miss a full understanding of our prophet's name. *Yonah* means "dove," and the word is used in the Noah story in Genesis 8. In that story, Noah sends the dove three times to look for land. Once it comes back with nothing. The second time it comes back with a "plucked-off olive leaf" (Genesis 8:11). The third time it does not return. The dove represents the possibility of a new beginning. From its first venture, the dove returns, having failed to find land. The dove succeeds on its second try. Our Yonah also succeeds only on his second try.

The story of Nineveh and the Noah story of the flood both involve a group of people who have become so evil that God decides to destroy them. Both stories involve trips over the water in boats, which is rare in Hebrew Bible stories. The other prominent example is the basket into which Yocheved places Moses in the Nile, and that narrative, like both the Jonah story and the Noah story, is a story of redemption.

The text tells us that Jonah is ben Amittai, the son of Amittai. *Amittai* derives from the Hebrew word *emet*, which means truth. Jonah then is the son of truth. Abarbanel says, "And because people always believe in the truth of his words he is called Ben Amittai," the son of truth. Is Jonah really a person of truth? He only reveals his story to the sailors when they cast lots and the lot falls on him. Generally he hides from the truth or denies it, as we will see most fully in chapter 4 of Jonah. Ben Amittai, indeed, is an ironic name for Jonah.

Since I was a child I have been amused by ironic names. Curly Howard was the bald member of the Three Stooges. Curly Neal was the bald member of the Harlem Globetrotters. Tiny Mills was a huge wrestler. And Jonah, the son of truth, is a liar.

What do we know about Jonah as the story begins? The book opens, "And the word of the Eternal came to Jonah son of (ben) Amittai." The biblical text does not introduce Jonah or provide us with any background about who Jonah is or why God is speaking to him. Does God regularly speak to Jonah? Is this the first time God has spoken to him? What name/s has Jonah earned before the events described in his biblical book?

Ibn Ezra and Kimchi provide context by drawing our attention to the other mention of Jonah in the Bible. From them we learn that Jonah was already an active prophet before his story begins. Ibn Ezra says, "This is the prophet who prophesied to the king, Jeroboam ben Yoash, as is written about him, [the promise] that the Eternal had made through His servant, the prophet Jonah son of Amittai from Gat-hepher" (2 Kings 14:25).

Kimchi explains that "Gat-hepher was the name of his city." And it is in the portion [of the Land of Israel] of Zebulun as it is written [in Joshua's division of the Land of Israel, "The third lot emerged for the Zebulunites] . . . to Gat-hepher, to Eth-kazin" (Joshua 19:10–13). These comments tell us where and when Jonah lived.

Abarbanel provides a fuller backstory for Jonah by turning to midrash (Bereishit Rabbah 98:11). The prophet Elijah revives a widow's son who has recently died (1 Kings 17:19–22.) The biblical text does not include the name of the boy, but the midrash imagines that he is actually the young Jonah.

Abarbanel turns to another story of an unnamed biblical character. According to 2 Kings 9:1–3, the prophet Elisha appoints an unnamed person to anoint Yehu to be the ruler of the Northern Kingdom of Israel. Then the prophet Elisha summoned one of the disciples of the prophets and said to him, "Tie up your skirts, and take along this flask of oil and go to Ramoth-gilead. . . . Go and see Jehu son of Jehoshaphat. . . . Then take the flask of oil and pour some on his head, and say, 'Thus said, the Eternal: I anoint you king over Israel.'" In the midrash, rabbis identify this messenger as Jonah. Abarbanel, drawing on the midrash, knows that this unnamed prophet is Jonah. Abarbanel writes, "When the prophet Elisha will place upon him the task to prophesy and will send him to anoint Yehu ben Namshi."

So for Abarbanel, Jonah has a special relationship with God before the events described in the book of Jonah. And Jonah has a connection to God's main representatives of that time and that place, the prophets Elijah and Elisha. Jonah's very existence is due to a miracle performed by Elijah. Elijah stands out among all of God's servants in the Hebrew Bible. He alone avoids death, for when Elijah's time on earth concludes, God sends a chariot of fire to carry him away. Elisha, Elijah's apprentice and successor, regards Jonah as an appropriate agent to carry out God's will in anointing Yehu, a task originally assigned by God to Elijah (1 Kings 19:16).

Abarbanel's explanation of Jonah's background would cause one to believe that Jonah has been and would continue to be a loyal servant of God. He offers no explanation for Jonah's disobedience to the Divine will. Rabbi Simeon said, "There are three crowns: the crown of Torah, the crown of priesthood, and the crown of kingship. But the crown of a good name excels them" (Pirke Avot 4:17). Abarbanel portrays Jonah as earning this crown of a good name. But this is not how most people imagine him; most see him as the prophet who defied God, ran away, and was swallowed by a big fish.

As we continue to read the narrative with the commentators, we will come to understand that their portrayal of Jonah varies greatly from the popular image. Some defend Jonah as a flawed prophet who has a legitimate reason for his misdeeds. Abarbanel goes further and considers Jonah a hero, willing to sacrifice his own life in order to save the lives of the people of the Northern Kingdom of Israel.

The Hebrew poet Zelda's best-known poem, *L'Chol Ish Yeish Shaim*, develops the theme stated in the midrash mentioned at the beginning of this chapter: we each have many names. Our identity comes from within and without. Zelda begins her poem: "Every person has a name / that God gave him / and which his father and mother gave him" and "Every person has a name / which his sins gave him, / and which his longing gave him."

The central figure in our story received the name Yonah ben Ammittai from his parents and the name "prophet" from God when God called on him to carry the Divine message to the Israelites and to the Ninevites. As we follow the thread of the story, we will examine the meanings found by others who have studied this story over the centuries. And as we read, we will discover who Jonah is and perhaps who we are.

2

Understanding the Other

Who Are They?

Go at once to Nineveh. —JONAH 1:2

Why does God send Jonah to deliver a message to the residents of a non-Israelite city? All the other biblical prophets are sent by God to speak to the people of Judah or Israel. What's more, Nineveh is not just any non-Israelite city; it is the capital of the Assyrian Empire, the enemy of Israel and Judah.

Nineveh raises broader questions: How do we view people different from ourselves? How do we as Jews look at non-Jews? Do we view non-Jews as hostile to Jews?

Many Jews see the "other" as the "threatening foreign other"; they look at the world mainly through the prism of the Holocaust and two thousand years of Jewish suffering. Some evaluate all events as "good for the Jews or bad for the Jews." While we may see our neighbors as gentiles, or the more pejorative Goyim, non-Jews do not think of themselves as non-Jews. Viewing members of the general population as "non-Jews" places us at the center of the human solar system, with the rest of humanity revolving around us.

In their comments about the phrase "Go at once to Nineveh," Abarbanel and Malbim present a human history that is centered on Jewish people. For them the Assyrian Empire is a supporting actor, because as they see it, the purpose of Jonah's mission to Nineveh is to prepare the Assyrian Empire for the role it will play in the destruction of the ten northern tribes in the Kingdom of Israel. Malbim explicitly says that this process of prophecy and repentance is not for the benefit of the Ninevites.

In his novel *Sirens of Titan*, Kurt Vonnegut tells of Salo, from the planet Tralfamadoria, who is stuck on Titan, a moon of Saturn, waiting for a replacement part for his spaceship. The Tralfamadorians manipulate human history to send messages to Salo. The Tralfamadorians cause Earthlings to build major structures that Salo can see through his telescope on Titan. These accomplishments of humanity spell out messages in the Tralfamadorian language. Stonehenge spells out "Replacement part being rushed with all possible speed." The Great Wall of China says, "Be patient. We haven't forgotten you." As Vonnegut suggests that these immense human projects were not actually constructed for earthly purposes, so the commentators suggest that the Assyrian campaign of conquest was not to meet Assyrian goals.

Abarbanel writes:

> It had been directed that because of their sins, the Kingdom of Israel, Samaria and her daughters would be destroyed by the hands of Assyria. Therefore the Blessed One tries to save Assyria from the evil that has been designated to come upon them as a result of their violence so that He will save Assyria from annihilation. And Assyria will become the instrument of the anger of the Holy One of Blessing to destroy [the Northern Kingdom of] Israel as it is written, "Ha! Assyria the rod of My anger [In whose hand, as a staff, is My fury!] I send him against an ungodly nation, I charge him against a people that provokes Me, / To take its spoil and seize its booty / And to make it a thing trampled / Like the mire of the street" (Isaiah 10:5). And because of this the Holy One of Blessing wants to straighten out Nineveh, the capital city of the Kingdom of Assyria. And this is the reason that he sent Jonah to proclaim upon it.

Malbim writes:

> So that they [the Ninevites] will return in repentance. The mission of Jonah was not for the benefit of the people of Nineveh. For we have not found [another case in which] the Eternal sent a

prophet from Israel to cause idolaters to return in repentance. . . . Rather [God's] concern for Nineveh is [really out of concern] for Israel. After [Jonah's prophecy] Assyria will be prepared to be a rod of the Eternal's anger to punish Israel who have obligated who deserve punishment themselves to God. The Eternal wants to cause the Assyrians to return in repentance so that they will be ready to fulfill His decree on Israel. And so that the cynic will not ask why did [God choose the] faithless [Assyrians] to uproot [the Israelites, it would seem to be] evil [people] destroying those more righteous than themselves. The Eternal wanted to demonstrate that Assyria possesses greater merit than Israel. For they hearken to the words of the prophet and repent. And Israel stiffens their necks [to avoid] hearkening [to the call of the] prophets.

In contrast to Abarbanel and Malbim, Kimchi does not present the Assyrians as bit players in the story of Israel. Kimchi sees the purpose of God sending Jonah to Nineveh as a teaching opportunity. He suggests that God has a message for the Israelites, a message for the Ninevites, and a message for all of humanity.

The message for the Israelites:

We are able to explain that it was written to be a moral lesson to Israel. Behold a foreign nation that is not a part of Israel was close to repentance and the first time that a prophet rebuked them they turned to a complete repentance from evil. And what about Israel, whom the prophets rebuke from dawn until dark, and still they do not turn from their evil?

The message for the Ninevites:

And also to make known to Nineveh the great wonder which the God, Who is Blessed, performed that Jonah was in the belly of the fish for three days and three nights and lived.

The message for all of humanity:

And also to teach that the God, Who is Blessed, is merciful to those who repent from any nation and grants them mercy even more so when they are many. [The last verse of the book of Jonah (4:11) explains that Nineveh contains 120,000 people.]

Ibn Ezra also does not accept this view of the Assyrians as incidental players. His reading of the text expresses an important theological position that we would not expect to find in a twelfth-century source. Through a creative interpretation of the text, Ibn Ezra sees the Ninevites at the center of their own story: "For there [in chapter 3 of the book of Jonah] we find the verse 'It was a large city to God.'" Ibn Ezra uses this verse to explain the verse here in chapter 1. Both verses describe Nineveh as "a great city" (*ir gedola*). The difference between them is that in chapter 3 the words "to God" (*Lailohim*) are added. Ibn Ezra asks why the text uses the words "to God" to describe Nineveh. Could the text not simply have described Nineveh as a "great city" without including "to God"? Ibn Ezra concludes that these words are in the text to tell us "that they [the Ninevites] already feared the Eternal from before" the time of Jonah. He contends that the Ninevites were not idol worshipping polytheists but rather monotheists who worshipped the Eternal.

Ibn Ezra continues to seek a clear understanding of this passage from the third chapter: "And it is written, 'All the nations are as naught in His sight. [He counts them as less than nothing]' (Isaiah 40:17). And there is no concern if they were many." This verse from Isaiah teaches that God does not care about the number of nonbelievers, for "He counts them as less than nothing." Therefore the fact that here God describes Nineveh as a large city and in Jonah 4:11 God specifically says that Nineveh is "that great city, in which there are more than a hundred and twenty thousand persons" demonstrates that the inhabitants were not in the category of "All the nations," not pagans. Following the Isaiah verse, if they were pagans, God would not count them. And to Ibn Ezra, the fact that God counts them as many proves that they had a prior relationship with God.

Ibn Ezra here argues that "a great city to God" does not describe the size of Nineveh but rather its importance to God:

And the explanation [of the Hebrew word] *Lailohim* is that they had been fearers of the Eternal in earlier days. Only now in the days of Jonah did they begin to do evil. If they had not originally been people of the Eternal, a prophet would not have been sent to them. And here we saw a complete repentance with nothing like it. And we do not find it written that they broke the altars of Baal or cut down idols.

If they had been idol worshippers turning for the first time to the worship of the One God, their complete repentance would have included the destruction of the places of idol worship. Chapter 3 includes a detailed description of the steps the people of Nineveh took to repent from their evil. There is no mention of destroying altars to idols. So Ibn Ezra concludes, "From this we can learn that they were not idol worshippers." They were worshippers of the same One God worshipped by the Israelites.

Why does God send Jonah to deliver a message to the residents of this non-Israelite city? According to Ibn Ezra, they merit God's attention and a visit from God's prophet because of their long-term, ongoing connection to God.

How to approach religions other than our own is a key question of our time. Do we sometimes look at "others" as threatening? Can we accept that people of other religious communities can be in a proper relationship with the same One God we serve, even though they use different images and tell different stories about that God's connection to humanity?

Many of us in the twenty-first century are ready to embrace religious pluralism. Finding a foundation for this approach in Ibn Ezra's twelfth-century commentary should strengthen our confidence in this view. Rather than placing the Jewish people at the center of the human solar system, we can imagine the Jewish people as one of the peoples in orbit around the One God at the center of all that exists.

3

Coming to Terms with Violence

What Is Evil?

For their wickedness has come before Me. —JONAH 1:2

The text does not explain this wickedness (*rah*) that has drawn God's attention to Nineveh. What have the Ninevites done to cause God to take note of their behavior? We cannot say that God is angry at the Ninevites for worshipping idols. Idol worship would not have been a unique sin on the part of the Ninevites because all of the Israelites' neighbors worshipped idols. But we can be certain that these undefined crimes of the Ninevites were severe. This is only the third time in the Bible in which the evil of a people moves God to speak of destroying them. The others are the generation of Noah and the people of Sodom and Gomorrah.

Kimchi writes, "We [can] learn [from this verse] that the God, Who is Blessed, takes note of sins of the nations of the world when their evil grows in violence (*chamas*)." *Chamas* is not a synonym for *rah*. It is a technical term for a specific category of evil. The Torah uses *chamas* to describe the evil of the generation of Noah and of the people of Sodom.

Kimchi continues, "And so it is in the generation of Noah and in the people of Sodom. And the violence destroys the community. And God, Who is Blessed, is concerned about all the communities in the world." In both of these cases God takes note of the sins of non-Israelites. God punishes the humanity of Noah's time by wiping them out. God rains fire down upon Sodom and Gomorrah. Here God designates the residents of Nineveh for the same fate. According to Kimchi, God becomes concerned about the sins of the other nations when they rise in severity and cross the *chamas* threshold.

One big difference between the Bible's description of Jonah's time and of Noah's time is that in the Jonah story God sends a prophet to warn the people, thereby giving them a second chance. The lack of prophetic warning to the Noah's generation bothered the ancient rabbis; they imagined that Noah himself warned the people, as in this midrash on "Make yourself an ark of gopher wood" (Genesis 6:14):

> Rabbi Huna said in the name of Rabbi Yosi: For one hundred and twenty years, God kept warning the generation of the flood in the hope that they would repent from their sins. When they did not repent, He said to Noah, "Make thee an ark of gopher wood." Noah proceeded to plant gopher trees. When asked, "What are these gopher trees for?" Noah would reply, "God is about to bring a flood upon the world, and He told me to make an ark, that I and my family might escape." The people mocked and ridiculed him. In the meantime the gopher kept growing.
>
> When again they asked, "What are you doing?" he gave the same answer. Finally when the trees had grown to maturity he cut the gopher trees down and sawed them into planks. Again the people asked, "What are you doing?" Noah again explained to the people about the coming flood. During the years that it took Noah to build the ark people asked, "What are you doing?" Noah again explained to the people about the coming flood. When the people still did not repent, God brought the flood upon them. At last when they realized that they were about to perish, they tried to break into the ark. What did God do then? He surrounded it with lions. (*Tanhuma*, Pashat *Noach*)

In this midrash by Rabbi Huna, quoting Rabbi Yosi, God uses Noah as a prophet to warn the people of his generation repeatedly for many years of the coming consequence of their sinful, violent ways. Rabbi Yosi has Noah taking his time building the ark in order to provide as much time as possible to warn the people. Rather than having Noah cut down already grown trees, Rabbi Yosi has Noah begin the ark by planting slow growing cedar trees and waiting for them to reach maturity.

Despite all of Noah's warnings, the people do not repent, and God destroys them. Here in our story, Jonah speaks four words of prophecy once, the people fully repent, and God forgives them. The difference is not in the message or the messenger but in the sinners. The people of Nineveh are different from the generation of the flood.

The flood story features truly evil people. In contrast, the Ninevites are good people who perform evil acts, and such people can reform. But truly evil people are beyond saving because they have lost the ability to distinguish between right and wrong. The generation of the flood ignored Noah. The people of Nineveh harkened to the warning delivered by Jonah.

In the media we see stories of athletes cheating by using performance-enhancing drugs, business people taking advantage of insider information, and religious leaders and coaches sexually abusing young people. Are these totally evil people who cannot distinguish right from wrong? These stories challenge our confidence in our fellow human beings. We want to make sense out of how normal people can perform evil acts. We do not want to think that humans are inherently evil.

We can think of many examples in popular culture that wrestle with this question of evil. We like the "honorable" gangsters and outlaws, like the Corleone family, Pretty Boy Floyd, and Robin Hood. They live by a code of honor. While the mobsters' code may not be exactly like medieval chivalry, it does set clear limits to define right and wrong.

This is not the *chamas*, the rampant violence of the generation of the flood. Some people who have committed crimes can turn a corner and redeem themselves. It can be difficult, but it does happen. I have seen it.

In recent years we have witnessed violent acts with no regard to any code of behavior. Individuals have taken powerful weapons into schools or and movie theaters to shoot as many people as they can.

They view their victims as objects rather than as human beings. This is *chamas*, the crime of the generation of the flood. These shooters have lost all sense of the "other" as having any value. They cannot respond to Noah's prophecy.

While some people in our midst may be so far gone that they have lost their sense of right and wrong, most people on the wrong path are not that far gone. They can still turn their lives around. They can still benefit from hearing the voice of the prophet reminding them, calling them to return. It is not too late for them. We will see that the people of Nineveh have not totally lost their sense of right and wrong. When Jonah points out their sins, they can hear his voice and change their lives. The challenge for us is to distinguish in our lives between those people who can be saved and those who are beyond saving.

In my work as a rabbi I have encountered people in both groups. When I was a young rabbi, I innocently believed I could save everybody. A young man of the congregation presented as a bit odd, not dangerous but a bit unusual. Often he would visit the synagogue to "meditate." He would sit in the lobby and softly chant. Some of the members of staff wanted me to tell him to go away. I argued that the synagogue provided a safe haven for this odd but harmless young man.

One day he came to my office, clearly aggravated. He told me that the police were after him. I called a member of the congregation who was a lawyer and asked him to help. He spoke to the police, and the police agreed to rescind the arrest order if the young man would check himself into a mental health facility. He did so, and he avoided arrest. After the arrest order was rescinded, he checked out of the hospital. Later I learned more details about the incident that had led to the arrest order. That morning, when he had gone to the hospital for treatment, he had opened his pants and exposed himself to staff and patients. I had helped him avoid facing the consequences of his actions. That day I learned the term *enabler*. Now I know that when things appear to be odd, they usually are. I have learned to focus my energies on aiding people who I can actually help grow and change, rather than letting myself get entangled in the shenanigans of people seeking to avoid the consequences of their actions.

The generation of the flood had descended to *chamas*. No amount of prophecy could save them. The people of Nineveh were doing *rah,* wickedness, but could still be saved. We face the challenge of distinguishing between *rah* and *chamas* in the world in which we live. We should not allow ourselves to get caught up in the lives of those who have descended to the level of *chamas*. We cannot help them. We should devote ourselves to helping the people struggling with *rah*. They still have an opportunity to change.

4

〰〰〰〰〰〰〰〰〰〰〰〰〰〰〰〰〰〰〰〰〰〰〰〰〰〰〰〰〰〰〰〰〰

Appreciating Context

What Makes Jonah Run?

Jonah, however, started out to flee to Tarshish
from the Eternal's service. —JONAH 1:3

Why does Jonah flee? Why does Jonah reject God's call to go to
Nineveh? Many biblical prophets express doubts when God calls
them. When God calls Amos to be a prophet, Amos responds, "I
am not a prophet, and I am not a prophet's disciple. I am a cattle
breeder and a tender of sycamore figs" (Amos 7:14). When God calls
to Jeremiah, he responds, "Ah, Sovereign God, I don't know how to
speak; For I am still a boy" (Jeremiah 1:6). Even Moses expresses
doubts (Exodus 3:11). But it is only Jonah who runs away.

How could Jonah have done such a thing? How could he have run
away from God? How could a prophet respond to God's call in such
a disrespectful manner? The obvious explanation is that Jonah fled
because he was afraid of what would happen to him if he did what
God had asked of him. He was afraid that if he went to Nineveh, the
Ninevites would kill him. Or perhaps the Ninevites would torture
and then kill him.

The commentators offer a variety of explanations for Jonah's flight.
They appear to be searching for a rationale, that there must be a
logical explanation for Jonah's reaction. They ask us to look beyond
the obvious, to see the hidden reason for Jonah's flight, to find his
good intentions.

Kimchi tells us that Jonah fled to avoid embarrassing the Israelites. God regularly sent prophets to speak to the Israelites, but they
always ignored these prophets:

How would he be able to flee? And when he was summoned to go on this mission, Jonah said to himself, the gentiles are close to repentance, and if I go on this mission, the God, Who is Praised, will turn them from their evil paths. And Israel will be accused by this [action]. For I, and other prophets, constantly come to them on a mission from the God, Who is Blessed, and they do not turn from their evil path. Therefore he did not accept this mission. Thus is the explanation of the sages of blessed memory [in the Mechilta to Parshat Bo]. Because of this it was impossible for him to accept his mission. . . . And since the gentiles are close to repentance and he did not want to obligate Israel [to punishment for being unwilling to repent], therefore he fled.

Abarbanel suggests that Jonah fled to avoid helping an enemy:

And here Jonah understands the truth of this matter and therefore concludes in his heart that he will not go to Nineveh so that the people of Assyria will not be saved from destruction by him. For what would be a reason for his going [to Nineveh] to save the children of Assyria and cut off the children of Israel? How would he be able to fear the evil that would befall his nation at the hands of the Assyrians and because of that flee from before the Eternal? That would be to say that he wished to distance himself from the Land of Israel the base for prophecy, in his thought that prophecy does not extend to outside the Land [of Israel]. And when he would be in an impure land outside the Holy Land, prophecy would not begin within him. And he would not be commanded to go to Nineveh. And [he would] not [have] to proclaim upon it the proclamation so that he would not be central to and an instrument in the saving of his enemy. And if Hashem of Blessing would want to save them He could do it Himself as He wished but not by the means of Jonah and by his hand.

Abarbanel explains that Jonah placed the honor of the people of Israel over the honor of God. He portrays Jonah as a hero sacrificing himself for the benefit of the people of Israel. "Jonah sought the honor of the son and did not seek the honor of the father. . . . As it is written in the midrash, Rabbi Yochanon said, Jonah did not go except to lose his life at sea." As it is written, "Heave me overboard" (Jonah 1:12). Jonah fled expecting that this would cost him his life.

In the *Wizard of Oz* after Toto has revealed "the man behind the curtain," Dorothy says to the Wizard, "Oh, you're a very bad man!" The Wizard responds, "Oh, no, my dear. I'm a very good man. I'm just a very bad wizard." The commentators seem to be saying that Jonah was a very good man, just a very bad prophet. Why did the commentators feel a need to defend Jonah?

They are participants in a broader conversation, but we only get to read their side of the conversation. The commentators wrote in response to voices with which we are not familiar, to the commentaries of Theodore of Mopsuestia, Jerome, and other early Christian writers. Writing in the fourth and fifth centuries, these Church Fathers argued the superiority of Christianity over Judaism. To them Jonah represents inferior, nationalistic Judaism in contrast to the universal faith of Christianity.

They argued that Jonah refused to go to Nineveh because he was angry that God expressed concerns for the non-Israelite Ninevites. They contend that as Jonah believed God should care only about Israelites, so Jews believe that God should only care about Jews. They contrast this particularistic position with their universal Christian image of God caring for all people. Cyril of Alexandria, in his commentary on Jonah, quotes from Paul's Epistle to the Romans, "Or is God the God of Jews only? Is he not the God of Gentiles, too? Yes, of Gentiles, too" (Romans 3:29).

Gregory of Nazianzus, a fourth-century archbishop of Constantinople, explains Jonah's flight: "He saw the fall of Israel, and understood that the grace of prophecy would pass to the nations. This is what leads him to withdraw from preaching and delay the execution of his mission." Jonah wants God to speak only to the people of Israel and only through Israelite prophets.

While the Jewish commentators do not refer directly to these Christian polemics, they offer more positive motivations for Jonah's flight. The medieval Jewish commentators lived at a time when Jews felt pressure to defend the validity of Judaism. Because we live in a more pluralistic, post-polemic society, we do not expect the interpretations of Jonah to be a battleground for an interfaith debate. But by understanding the historical context, we have greater insight into the commentators' efforts to put a positive spin on Jonah's flight.

The commentators read the text in the context of their lives, and we read the text in the context of our lives. I am aware that I see the world through Jewish eyes. I notice if a baseball player has a Jewish name. The Chicago Cubs delight me when they sign a Jewish player. The team disappoints me when they trade a Jewish player to another team. What we notice is not what another person notices.

Bach's music all sounds the same to me. I cannot distinguish one piece from another. But if someone said to me, "Like a Rolling Stone" is just another Bob Dylan song and all Bob Dylan's songs sound the same, I would respond indignantly. What do you mean? "Like a Rolling Stone" is not just another Bob Dylan song. It changed the world. I could go on and on about Dylan going electric at the Newport Folk Festival in the summer of 1965.

I know very little about Bach's compositions but a great deal about Dylan's music. I am familiar with the dramatic and subtle shifts in Dylan's songs over the years. While I may not be a leading expert on the songs of Bob Dylan, I certainly know them well. I can speak about his songs in light of the context of when he wrote them. I can discuss what his oldest songs meant in the context of the sixties and what they mean today. We can now more fully understand the commentators' explanations of Jonah's flight now that we know that they wrote them as a response to the Church Fathers.

Often we do not fully understand those who speak to us because we do not grasp their context. We may become frustrated and angry because others do not seem to understand us. We speak past each other rather than to each other. This dynamic may result from political or cultural differences.

We should not dismiss the words of others that do not make sense to us. Rather we should strive to understand that the context of their lives may provide meaning to their words.

5

Descent and Salvation

How Low Can You Go?

. . . he went down to Joppa. —JONAH 1:3

Jonah could have gone to hide in a mountain cave like Rabbi Shimon Bar Yochai did later in the second century, during the Hadrianic persecution. Jonah could have gone north to the Golan Heights, up to Mount Hermon to flee from God. But Jonah did not hide in a cave or go to the mountains: he ran toward the sea. The Bible describes the first steps of Jonah's flight as a descent.

Kimchi explains:

> [Jonah could have gone down to Jaffa] from his city which was Gat-hepher or from Jerusalem. [In either case he would be starting in the mountains.] And he went down to Jaffa that was on the shore of the sea. And it is a ship harbor. And those who enter the sea are described as those "who go down." As it says, "Others go down to the sea in ships" (Psalms 107:23). For the shore of the sea is a low area, its elevation is at sea level as compared to the rest of the dry land. My father, of blessed memory, [Rabbi Joseph Kimchi], said that the explanation of why the word *going down* is used in connection with ships is that the ship is deep and one goes down into it. As it says, "He found a ship . . . and went down into it" (Jonah 1:3). And therefore it says, "Jonah went down into the hold of the vessel" (Jonah 1:50). And thus [the verse from Psalms 107:23 says], "Others go down to the sea in ships."

Kimchi's comments stress Jonah's step-by-step descent.

Abarbanel comments: "The land of Israel is higher than all the other lands." When one moves to Israel, it is said that one is making *aliyah,* going up. An Israeli who has left the Land of Israel has made *yerida*, descent. In the Jewish imagination, the Land of Israel is, as Abarbnel says, higher than all other lands. So by leaving the Land of Israel, Jonah descends from the heights.

Leaving the Land of Israel is only one step in Jonah's descent. After he climbs down into the ship, he continues to descend. We read, "Jonah had gone down into the hold of the vessel" (Jonah 1:5). He moves still lower when the sailors throw him into the sea. Later, in chapter 2:7, Jonah goes even lower, when he is in the belly of the fish; as it says, "I sank to the base of the mountains." The fish carries Jonah to the bottom of the sea.

What does the author of Jonah wish to convey with this description of Jonah's continuing descent?

In the Bible, encounters with God often take place on mountaintops. God instructs Abraham to offer Isaac as a sacrifice on Mount Moriah (Genesis 22: 2). God appears to Moses in the burning bush on a mountain, "Horeb, the mountain of God" (Exodus 3:1). God gives Moses the Torah on Mount Sinai (Exodus 19:20). Solomon builds the Temple in Jerusalem on what we call the Temple Mount (1 Kings 6:1). Elijah confronts the prophets of Ba'al on Mount Carmel (1 Kings 18:20). In the Bible, as well as in the western religious imagination, God is up. In my teaching I can point up to refer to God, confident that everyone will understand the gesture. As Jonah descends to the depths of the sea, he moves farther away from God.

This metaphor of up and down continues to function in our contemporary secular society. A sad person might say, "I feel down." The Beatles sang, "I'm down, I'm really down. How can you laugh when you know I'm down?" (Lennon-McCartney). Later, in a contrasting song they sang, "I get high with a little help from my friends" (Lennon-McCartney). We describe an enterprise that is not what it used to be as "going downhill." We use a boxing metaphor to describe a person who is done: "down for the count." We want to be up, not down.

Sometimes when we feel down in the dumps, it is because we are literally or metaphorically in the wrong place. We feel far from where we wish to be. Jonah, hiding in the hold of the ship, is far from God. He feels "all alone, without a home, a complete unknown" (Bob Dylan) in the hold of the ship. But Jonah is not on his own. God has not given up on him. God could have said, "If you want to run, run. Who needs you? I have better prophets than you that I can send to Nineveh. You have a good time in Tarshish. I will send Elisha, another prophet, to Nineveh."

But that is not how God responds to Jonah's flight. God does not wait for Jonah to turn back. In verse 4 we will see that God takes the first step in drawing Jonah back to Divine service.

In Rashi's commentary to this verse we read, "The Holy One of Blessing said to him, 'By your life! I have agents like you whom I can send after you to retrieve you from there.'" Jonah is not the only player on God's roster. God has other players on the bench who can be sent into the game.

Rashi continues, "An illustration [of this principle can be seen in the story of] a servant of a priest who ran away from his master and entered a cemetery [which priests are prohibited from entering]. His master said to him, 'I have servants like you whom I can send after you to retrieve you from there.'" God's power does not end at the edge of the Land of Israel. God has other means, such as the storm and then the fish, to retrieve Jonah. God directs the fish to take Jonah to the very bottom of the sea, before He begins to draw Jonah back up. We can think of those who retrieved us from our deepest depths.

In 1986 I traveled to the Soviet Union with my friend Mike to visit Jewish activists. In Leningrad (today St. Petersburg) we met with Anna. Her husband had been arrested for anti-Soviet slander, and the government had sent him to a prison camp on the Kamchatka peninsula, at the other end of the Soviet Union. Her son Boris was in an army hospital in Archangel. We brought items she could sell on the black market. She shared with us the newest detail of her situation so that we could report to those working on her behalf in the United States. During our visit, Anna's ten-year-old daughter, Masha, asked me where my family came from. I told her that my grandparents left Lithuania before World War I. Masha asked her mother, "Why were his grandparents smarter than mine? Why did mine stay here?" Ever since that day I have understood that I was saved from the harshness of life in the Soviet Union by the decisions of my grandparents.

During the deepest depths of my struggles, a friend helped me climb out. In the fall of 1969 when I should have been a sophomore at the University of Minnesota, I was living in Hyde Park on the south side of Chicago with some friends from Habonim Labor Zionist Youth. They were all students at the University of Chicago. Most of them were in pre-med. I was doing very little. I had flunked out of school the previous spring because I had stopped going to class. I was "down" in every way.

The only thing that kept me off the streets was the kindness of my friends. I was doing a little work helping out with Habonim youth programs. One weekend in late October I went to a farm outside Madison, Wisconsin, to staff a program. My friend Sam drove down from Minneapolis to see me. He spoke to me in his usual enthusiastic manner. He helped me see that I was nowhere, doing nothing, but that it didn't have to be that way.

I went back to Minneapolis with him. We got an apartment, and I got a part-time job. The university was willing to let me try again. I took advantage of my second chance at the "U." I went to class and took my studies seriously. I graduated on time and went on to rabbinic school at the Hebrew Union College.

God used a storm and a fish to save Jonah. My friend Sam's effort got me back on the path to a productive and meaningful life. He saved me.

6

Overcoming Uncertainty

How Should I Act?

Vayiten S'charah, He paid its fare. —JONAH 1:3

In the late 1970s my wife, Tammie, and I visited her grandfather in Kassel, Germany. We took a bus to the center of the city, and as we boarded we tried to pay the driver. He shook his head. Later as we left the bus we tried to pay the driver, and again he shook his head. Later in the day we told Tammie's grandfather how we couldn't pay for our bus ride. He explained that there was a machine on a post at the bus stop from which we should have purchased our tickets. These days we would have recognized such a machine right away, but in 1978 it was new technology that we didn't even notice.

Once he found a ship in Jaffa harbor to take him to Tarshish, how did Jonah know the correct way to pay for his passage? Kimchi offers three explanations:

1) "The payment that he saw as appropriate to give" to the agent collecting money.
2) "He [the agent] told him [Jonah] to give [him the money]."
3) All the passengers followed the custom and "gave it [the payment] at the beginning [of the voyage]." And Jonah paid the same amount that the other passengers paid.

In social situations where we are comfortable and with people we know, we understand how to act. And in new situations that remind us of previous experiences, we understand what is expected of us. When we get to play a familiar role, we know what to do. When I get to be the "rabbi," I am at ease.

New social situations with people we do not know, in an unfamiliar setting, in which we lack defined roles, create anxiety. We do not know how to act, to whom we can speak, or what to say. In such situations I feel like I am on a roller coaster being pulled up the first incline approaching the crest, fearing the free fall. In these situations we can follow one of Kimchi's explanations of Jonah's actions. Those of us with James Bond–like self-confidence will just do what seems right. If we are lucky, someone will realize we are newcomers and tell us what to do. More often we will resort to looking at what others are doing and mimic their behavior.

How the text describes Jonah paying for his ship passage to Tarshish puzzles the commentators. The text could have said that Jonah paid *the* fare (*hasachar*) or *his* fare (*s'charo*), but the possessive suffix *ah* on "it is fare" (*s'charah*) causes the phrase to mean Jonah paid "*its* fare." Rashi explains, "He not only advanced [his own fare] but paid the charter rate." He concludes that the suffix *ah* indicates that Jonah paid for the whole boat, not just one seat. Ibn Ezra disagrees with Rashi. As is his usual approach, he seeks a simpler answer. Jonah did "not [pay] all of the cost [for the entire ship], but rather just what he was required to pay for his portion [for the cost of one person to travel from Jaffa to Tarshish]." Kimchi follows Rashi. He believes that Jonah is in a hurry to depart from the port of Jaffa.

During my student days in Jerusalem, to travel to Tel Aviv we could take the hourly bus or for only a bit more money take a *sheirut,* parked across the street from Jerusalem's main bus station. The *sheirut* drivers did not operate on a schedule; as soon as they sold all seven seats in the vehicle they would be on their way to Tel Aviv. The seventh passenger did not have to wait at all, but the first passenger might have to wait twenty to thirty minutes for the *sheirut* to fill up. Kimchi imagines the ships of the time and place functioning like a *sheirut*. Kimchi explains, "In the midrash [the text says] that he paid for the entire ship because he was in a hurry to go. And he did not consider [waiting for the ship to fill with] businessmen and women because he was in a hurry to leave (TB Nedarim 38a)."

Abarbanel brings a different understanding of the prevailing custom to paying for a journey. In our time we pay for flights months in advance knowing that the airline will transport us to our destination. The weather on the actual day of our flight may cause a delay of some hours, but nevertheless we will end up at our destination. In ancient times a successful voyage depended upon favorable winds, and so the captain could not guarantee that the ship would reach its intended destination. Abarbanel explains that passengers did not pay at the beginning of the voyage but only at its conclusion. "It was the way of seafarers not to pay the fare for the journey until they exit the ship to the port. Here Jonah, close to [fulfilling his] desire to escape, abandons the rest of his work in his boarding it [the ship]. Thus in the explanation in Pirke de Rebbi Eliezer, Jonah was wealthy and the entire ship [he chartered it] so that it would transport him alone." Jonah was anxious to get going. He was willing to pay upfront and buy all the seats.

Malbim gives a reason for Jonah's wanting to be alone on the ship. He portrays him as anticipating the rough seas that lay ahead and feeling concern for others. "And Jonah was in a hurry so he paid the price of the entire ship. And he had in this [desire to] hurry two intentions, so that the ship would leave immediately and so that there would not be found on the ship many people, for he knew that the passengers on the ship would be in danger and he did not want many souls to be lost."

Some people wait until everything is ready before they proceed. Others go right ahead, ready or not. Looking at it one way, it is a contrast between careful and reckless; from another, it is the difference between timid and bold. In Jonah's actions we can see the worst of both of these sets of choices. Jonah is too timid to go to Nineveh, but he flees recklessly. History and popular culture provide illustrations of the differing paths people follow.

In 1862 after the disaster of Bull Run, Gen. George McClellan was given command of the Army of the Potomac. All summer he requested more men and supplies, fearful about the size of Robert

E. Lee's Army of Northern Virginia. In truth the Union forces were much larger than Lee's. Frustrated by McClellan's inaction, President Lincoln is reported to have said, "If General McClellan isn't going to use his army, I'd like to borrow it for a time." McClellan's timidity dramatically limited his effectiveness as a military commander. Capt. James T. Kirk stands in stark contrast to General McClellan. Each episode of the original *Star Trek* television show began with Kirk describing the purpose of the starship *Enterprise*: "Space, the final frontier. These are the voyages of the starship *Enterprise*. Her five-year mission: to explore strange new worlds, to seek out new life and new civilizations, to boldly go where no one has gone before."

The civil rights movement in the 1950s and 1960s stands as a strong example of the value of bold action. In the early summer of 1963, the leaders of the civil rights movement were in our nation's capital preparing for the August March on Washington, very well aware that in April the police of Birmingham, Alabama, had responded violently to peaceful civil rights demonstrators. Rabbi Abraham Joshua Heschel was part of a delegation of religious leaders scheduled to meet with President John F. Kennedy at the White House on June 17 to seek his support for the civil rights movement. In advance of that meeting Heschel sent a telegram to Kennedy suggesting that the president act boldly in support of the movement.

I look forward to privilege of being present at meeting tomorrow. [The] likelihood exists that Negro problem will be like the weather. Everybody talks about it but nobody does anything about it. Please demand of religious leaders personal involvement, not just solemn declaration. We forfeit the right to worship God as long as we continue to humiliate Negroes. Church [and] synagogue have failed. They must repent. Ask of religious leaders to call for national repentance and personal sacrifice. Let religious leaders donate one month's salary toward fund for Negro housing and education. I propose that you, Mr. President, declare state of moral emergency.

A Marshall Plan for aid to Negroes is becoming a necessity. The hour calls for moral grandeur and spiritual audacity.

Jonah refused to journey to the unknown city of Nineveh. We can do better. We do not need to explore space. But rather than timidly moving from day to day, let us boldly live lives of moral grandeur and spiritual audacity.

7

Redirecting Lives

Which Way Does the Wind Blow?

But the Eternal cast a mighty wind upon the sea and such
a great tempest came upon the sea. —JONAH 1:4

Why does God send a "mighty wind" to create this "great tempest"?
God could have shut down the winds so that the ship carrying Jonah
would be becalmed. Samuel Taylor Coleridge depicts such a scene
in the *Rime of the Ancient Mariner:*

Day after day, day after day,
We stuck, nor breath nor motion;
As idle as a painted ship
Upon a painted ocean.
Water, water, every where,
And all the boards did shrink;
Water, water, every where,
Nor any drop to drink

The lack of wind afflicts the Ancient Mariner and his shipmates.
Like the sailors in our story, they fear that death awaits them.

Ibn Ezra explains that the wind is not just to bring about the storm
but also to keep those on the ship out to sea and away from dry land.
"[We should understand the phrase to mean that] He sent the storm
with a dual purpose. The verb *cast (haytil)* [is used] in the manner
of a metaphor. And the reason that he sent it from the land toward
the sea is so that they would not be able to return to the land." Ibn
Ezra suggests that the word *haytil* tells us that God sent the storm to
blow in a specific direction. Because we know that the sailors were
unable to bring the ship closer to the shore, we can conclude that the

winds and currents formed by the storm came from the direction of the land toward the open sea. "For it is not only the place where the sea joins with the river [presumably the Yarkon], it is close to the shore, a place that is always difficult for ships." The area close to shore presents many problems for safe navigation, including varying depths of the sea, changing tides, varying currents, and the rocks of the coast. "And the evidence for this [understanding of the text is in Jonah 2:4] as it says, 'You cast me into the depths, Into the heart of the sea, and the river whirled around me.'" Therefore this must have been a part of the sea close enough to the mouth of a river for there still to be a river current to "whirl around" Jonah.

We should pay close attention to how God responds to Jonah's flight. God does not prevent Jonah from leaving the Land of Israel, even though He could have rendered him unacceptable to any ship captain by afflicting him with leprosy, as He did to Miriam when she slandered Moses (Numbers 12:1–2).

Generally in the Bible's miracle stories God creates situations that allow for events to unfold in a certain way rather than directly intervening to change them. For example, in the book of Joshua we read of the battle with the Amorites. "On that occasion, when the Eternal routed the Amorites before the Israelites, Joshua addressed the Eternal; he said in the presence of the Israelites: 'Stand still, O sun, at Gibeon, O moon, over the Valley of Aijalon!' And the sun stood still, and the moon halted, while a nation wreaked judgment on its foe. . . . Thus the sun halted in the midheaven and did not press on to set for a whole day" (Joshua 10:12–13). Rather than directly causing the death of the Canaanite soldiers, God causes the sun to stand still over the valley of Aijalon, so that Joshua can complete his defeat of the Canaanites.

And in the book of Exodus, rather than lifting the Israelites out of Egypt, God sends plagues to persuade Pharaoh to free the Israelites, and then the Israelites themselves have to act to be saved; they must place the blood of the lamb on the doorposts of their homes. "Then Moses summoned all the elders of Israel and said to them,

'Go pick out lambs for your families and slaughter the Passover offering. Take a bunch of hyssop, dip it into the blood in the basin and apply some of the blood to the lintel and on the two doorposts. None of you shall go out of the door of his house until morning. For when the Eternal goes through to smite the Egyptians, He will see the blood on the lintel and the two doorposts, and the Eternal will pass over that door and not let the Destroyer enter and smite your home'" (Exodus 12:21–23). God created the circumstances that provided the opportunity for the Israelites to act to save themselves.

In the Jonah story God does not prevent Jonah from boarding the ship or prevent the ship from leaving the harbor. God does not pluck Jonah from the ship. God sends a wind and then allows events to unfold. God does not want to control Jonah like a puppeteer manipulating a marionette's strings, but rather provide an opportunity for Jonah to grow and mature, to learn to see himself as part of something larger. God wants to see Jonah's response to the storm that puts him and also the sailors at risk. God wants to see if Jonah can learn to care about others.

It is often said, "If you give a man a fish, you feed him for a day. Teach a man to fish, and you feed him for a lifetime." I find that oft-repeated wisdom is generally not as true as speakers claim. Simply teaching a person to do something does not necessarily mean that they will embrace it and make it part of their lives. We can teach people to fish, but if they have not taken ownership of fishing, they may never fish again. They may fish only when the teacher is watching. They may pretend to fish. Fishing may be contrary to their culture, religion, or way of life. Rather than "teaching the man to fish," create the circumstances that help people make their own decision to learn to fish. It is more likely that they will embrace it as their own.

It is generally not effective to tell someone, "You should . . ." Usually they will reject you and your advice. And even if they follow your advice, they may resent you for having given it. Have you made a change because someone told you to do so? Or have you learned from your own experience? We are often more effective by acting indirectly, by providing or shaping opportunities that will help others see the light. Sometimes it is best to remain silent even though we know the answer.

When I was a small child, bowling was a frustrating experience because my ball would often end up in the gutter. By the time I took my own children bowling, the bowling alley had bumpers we could use to prevent gutter balls and make bowling a more positive experience for children. We can be like these bumpers, waiting for the errant ball to come our way. Then we can gently redirect it. In our story God provides the storm to redirect Jonah.

8

Our Faith and Theirs

How Do We View Other Religions?

In their fright, the sailors cried out, each to his own god. —JONAH 1:5

The storm threatens sailors' ships and their lives. Prayer is a common and reasonable response to crisis. As Abarbanel explains, "The text says that the sailors in their fear of the storm cried out and called each to his god. That this is the first way [to save themselves] that people tried at the time of a storm." This approach grows out of the belief that such a severe storm must be an act of a deity in response to the misdeeds of a human being. Malbim writes, "Out of their fear each man cried out to his god in the belief that this anger came from the wrath of their god." Rashi, closely reading the text, is able to find another meaning. "Each man to his own god." This phrasing, in the singular, shows that the sailors did not share a common god but that each sailor had a different god. In fact, "every nationality of idolater was represented." The ship then becomes a microcosm for the entire gentile world.

Throughout rabbinic literature we find the concept that the world contains seventy nations. "On the Festival [Sukkot] Israel offers you seventy bullocks for the seventy nations of the world" (Bamidbar Rabbah 21.24). This idea grows out of the list of the seventy male descendants of Noah (Genesis 10:1–29). Knowing this, if the crew included a representative of every nation, the ship had a crew of seventy sailors.

The ancient rabbis argued that the prayers of sailors from seventy nations praying to seventy different gods did not produce results. The rabbis contend that they were not effective prayers because they were directed to the wrong address. Only prayers to the One God can be effective because only the One God is real.

In 1 Kings, chapter 18 we find the story of Elijah confronting the prophets of Ba'al on Mount Carmel. The prophets of Ba'al build an altar and pray to Ba'al to cause their sacrifice to ignite. When it fails to do so, Elijah engages in biblical trash talk. He taunts the prophets of Ba'al. He tells them they should speak up; perhaps Ba'al is sleeping. When Elijah's turn arrives to build his altar to the One God of Israel, he digs a moat around it, fills the moat with water, and then pours water on his altar three times. The One God of Israel sends a lightning bolt, which ignites the soaking wet sacrifice. The message is clear: the One God of Israel has power and Ba'al does not.

The ancient rabbis refer to the non-Jews as "star worshippers," the other nations as idolaters. This may seem harsh, but these anti-gentile polemics did not arise in a vacuum. They arose in response to pressure from the other religions. The biblical prophets denounce the Israelites for being drawn toward the worship of idols. We can be certain that this was a serious problem; otherwise, it would not have required so much attention; prophets do not bother denouncing the inconsequential.

The rise of Christianity brought pressure on Jews to convert to the new faith. Church authorities wrote polemics arguing the new faith superseded Judaism. They called upon Jews to give up their stubborn hold on an old religion. The later rise of Islam also brought pressure. While in many times and places Islamic authorities treated the Jews with kindness and respect, there were periods of serious pressure and threats. The fundamentalist Almohad dynasty in Spain and North Africa in the twelfth century demanded that Jews convert to Islam, and many Jews fled in response. Abraham Ibn Ezra left Spain for Italy; the parents of David Kimchi immigrated to Provence.

We saw in Ibn Ezra's comment on verse 2 an expression of medieval religious pluralism. He imagined that the Ninevites were not polytheistic idol worshippers but rather worshippers of the One God. And Rabbi Sholmo Riskin, a leading contemporary orthodox rabbi, has written, "The overwhelming majority of *halakhic* decisors during the past several hundred years see Christianity as idolatry for Jews, but not for Christians. For Jews, the trinity is a weakening of pure monotheism; however, for Christians who believe that the trinity is ultimately a unity and includes the one true God who created the Heavens and the Earth, this belief is a movement away from paganism and towards monotheism. It therefore cannot be considered idolatrous for the Christians" (*Jewish Week* 09/05/2012).

Until recently people of different religions rarely prayed together. My best friend could not attend my bar mitzvah in 1963. Bobby was our Catholic next-door neighbor, and in those days Catholics were not allowed to enter non-Catholic houses of worship. The past fifty years have seen big changes; in recent decades, popes have visited the synagogue in Rome.

In our day we engage followers of other religions. We make common cause. We join together to work for social change. We pray together. Many communities have an annual interfaith Thanksgiving service where Jews, Christians, Muslims, and others pray together. Many Christian denominations have in recent decades adopted positive official statements affirming the validity of Judaism. A case in point is "Nostra Aetate," a document that the Second Vatican Council adopted in 1965 proclaiming that the Jewish people have a living covenant with God. It explicitly condemns antisemitism and repudiates the charge that Jews bear any responsibility for the crucifixion of Jesus.

Many Protestant denominations have followed the lead of the Roman Catholic Church. For example, the Church Council of the Evangelical Lutheran Church in America on April 18, 1994, declared, "Grieving the complicity of our own tradition within this history of hatred, moreover, we express our urgent desire to live out our faith in Jesus Christ with love and respect for the Jewish people. We recognize in antisemitism a contradiction and an affront to the Gospel, a violation of our hope and calling, and we pledge this church to oppose the deadly working of such bigotry, both within our own

circles and in the society around us. Finally, we pray for the continued blessing of the Blessed One upon the increasing cooperation
and understanding between Lutheran Christians and the Jewish
community."

I teach Introduction to Bible at Elmhurst College, a United Church
of Christ liberal arts college. The course covers the Bible as defined
by Christians, which means that the students in my course learn
about the Gospel according to Matthew from a rabbi.

The journey toward a growing understanding between Jews and
Christians has hit a few bumps in the road. In 1980 Bailey Smith,
the president of the Southern Baptist Convention, rocked the interfaith world by declaring, "God Almighty does not hear the prayer
of a Jew." Obviously Jews objected, but so did many Baptists. Pastor
Michael Smith of First Baptist Church of Murfreesboro, Tennessee,
said, "His comment amazed and saddened me. . . . He seemed not
to realize that Jesus was a first-century Jew, as were all of his earli-
est followers. Certainly, God heard their prayers. In my opinion, he
also misunderstood the relationship between God and all humanity.
Whatever else might be said, the Bible teaches that we are made in
the image of God. Jesus compared God to a loving parent, who stands
ever ready to listen to his children. Such a God hears the prayers
of anyone." Since 1980 many Jewish–Baptist dialogue groups have
developed. Smith and Rabbi Rami M. Shapiro have written a two-
volume work, *Mount and Mountain*, in which they discuss the Ten
Commandments and the Sermon on the Mount.

The verse with which we began this chapter continues, "They
threw the ship's cargo overboard to make it lighter for them." Too
many of today's Jews look at Christians tainted by the memory of
centuries of Christianity's hostility. In light of the profound changes
that have taken place in recent decades, the time has come for us to
throw that cargo overboard. I do not mean to suggest that we should
forget about the Crusades, the Inquisition, and the Holocaust; of
course not. But those events of the past should not prevent us from
looking at the contemporary Christian world as it has shifted. It has

extended the hand of friendship toward us, and it is time for us to grasp that hand in friendship.

In our time Jews need to learn more about Christianity. In September 2000, 220 rabbis and intellectuals published the first major Jewish statement about the Jewish–Christian relationship, "*Dabru Emet*, Speak the Truth" Most Jews have a very limited understanding of Christianity. Most have never explored Christian religious texts. As we would like Christians to understand and respect Jews and Judaism, Jews must understand and respect Christians and Christianity.

9

Overcoming Despair

Why Does He Sleep So Deeply?

> He lay down and fell asleep. The captain went over
> to him and cried out, "How can you be sleeping so
> soundly? Up and call to your God." —JONAH 1:5–6

In verse 5 Jonah falls asleep. This verse is often read to mean that Jonah was already on board, sleeping in the hold when the storm began. Ibn Ezra sees it differently, that Jonah goes to sleep in order to hide "from the danger of the sea and His anger." Ibn Ezra suggests that "perhaps he did not enter the ship before this [storm began]." Perhaps the storm was already raging and Jonah sought sleep to escape the fury of the storm and God's anger.

Abarbanel adds, "The text says this to explain that as the sailors cried to their gods, Jonah did not cry out to Hashem, for he was embarrassed and ashamed to raise his face to Him. So 'He lay down and fell asleep' thinking that he would die there. For sleep is one-sixtieth of death, and so he prepared himself for it." Jonah sleeps in the hold of the ship, retreating from life. For Jonah the hold of the ship seems like a womb. He sleeps peacefully, oblivious to the chaos of the world around him.

Psychologists tell us that some people who suffer from despair or depression or are afraid of what's to come sleep to escape, and this could be what Jonah is doing. He could be going to sleep to escape the crisis.

Late one afternoon, when I was nineteen years old, I opened a letter from the University of Minnesota telling me that I was no longer a student; I had flunked out because I wasn't regularly going to classes. I went right to bed and didn't get up until the next morning, fourteen hours later. I scared my roommates. I clearly did not want to face the reality of that letter. I was frightened of how my parents would respond, and I was terrified of what action my draft board would take. I slept to avoid the real-life crisis before me.

On occasion nations seem to retreat into sleep to avoid facing clear and present dangers. In 1938 Winston Churchill published *While England Slept*, attacking the United Kingdom's lack of military preparation to face the threat of Nazi Germany's expansion.

Sleeping individuals, as well as sleeping nations, sometimes require an "alarm clock" to awaken them. Winston Churchill saw this as his role. In our story, the captain of the ship does not allow Jonah to continue to escape through sleep. He wakes Jonah up.

The Hebrew words that begin the captain's call to Jonah, "*Mah l'cha nirdam*," literally mean, "What is this to you, O sleeping one?" Rashi rephrases it as "How can you be sleeping? This is no time to sleep!" Abarbanel adds, "And it is as if he says to Jonah, 'Don't you see the difficulty of this moment and the great danger in which we stand? How can you not feel it?'"

Jonah is not on the boat all alone. The captain wakes Jonah so that he can help save the ship. Jonah's despair could cause greater damage than just damage to himself. The captain does not say to Jonah, "Wake up and save yourself!" Rather, the captain's message is "Wake up and perhaps you can save us!"

A famous midrash tells of another sea traveler impacting other passengers. A group of people were traveling in a boat when one of them took a drill and began to drill a hole beneath him. "Why are you doing this?" his companions said to him. "What concern is it of yours?" replied the man. "Am I not drilling under my own place?" And they replied to him: "But you will flood the boat for us all!" (Midrash Rabbah, Vayikra 4:6). In our story, Jonah's slumber could lead to the sinking of the ship.

People deep in despair do not need to hear that their despair is not real; they need to hear that they do not face their problem alone.

They need to hear that their despair impacts many people. They need to hear that they have the power to act, that they are more powerful than they imagine themselves to be. Abarbanel says that the captain explained to Jonah what to do: "And if you say that you do not know what to do, act like the sailors. Get up and call to your God. You know how to do that."

The first step in emerging from despair is to get up and see that you are still alive. With the support of others you can see that you are not the only one facing this kind of crisis. Then you'll have the wherewithal to confront your circumstances and your possibilities.

A.A. plays a powerful role in the lives of recovering alcoholics. "Alcoholics Anonymous® is a fellowship of men and women who share their experience, strength, and hope with each other that they may solve their common problem and help others to recover from alcoholism" (A.A. Mission Statement). It's a model for a wide variety of support groups, including a very unusual one, Illinois Parents of Murdered Children. I spoke to this group once, and at the beginning of the meeting each participant told his or her story of tragic loss. Sharing the stories did not lessen their pain, but shared experience did give them strength to face the "rough water."

Some people are fortunate enough to be part of a strong circle of friends or a close-knit community that is always there to provide support in difficult times. Active participants in strong, healthy congregations report such experiences. I see this in my congregation, and I hear about it happening in others as well.

Abarbanel suggests that the sailors, who had concluded that their prayers wouldn't stop the storm, saw Jonah's prayers as their last hope. Abarbanel writes, "And they did not yet know if the God of Jonah would be greater than all their gods. But they said, 'Perhaps the God of Jonah will pay mind to us and not destroy us.' They mean to say if our gods do not have the strength to save us, perhaps if we draw ourselves close to the God of Jonah and if we are united, He will be able to save us."

The sleeping Jonah, hiding in the hold of the ship, doesn't seem the least bit heroic. Rather he is engaged in a game of spiritual hide-and-seek. The captain finds him and wakes him, hoping that maybe Jonah's prayers will be their salvation. In the next verse Jonah's role in the storm begins to become clear to everybody on board.

10

Fate and Free Will

What Path Will We Follow?

Let us cast lots and find out on whose account this misfortune has
come upon us. They cast lots and the lot fell on Jonah. —JONAH 1:7

Having thrown cargo overboard and having prayed, why did the sailors take this unusual step of casting lots? And why did the sailors
believe that casting lots would yield the truth?

Abarbanel writes: "And when the sailors saw that their prayer and
their outcry were not effective and also that the lightness of the ship
which resulted from them throwing the cargo into the sea [did not
improve their situation], they thought that this storm was a matter
set by God because of the suffering of one of them. And it is not
proper that a person should think that the sailors threw Jonah into
the sea in haste and in a hurry. For they relied on experiences to
prove that this storm was not natural [but rather it is] in the way of
God's oversight [of the world]."

Kimchi comments on the unusual qualities of this storm:

There is something puzzling in this matter. Why did they think
that on account of the men of this ship the Eternal sent this big storm
to the sea? Weren't there other ships in the sea? And do the crews of
all ships that are in a storm at sea cast lots to learn on whose account
the evil falls on them? I found in Pirke de Rebbi Eliezer (chapter 10)
[an explanation of how this storm in the book of Jonah was different from the storms that sailors regularly encounter]. A great storm
came upon them in the sea. But to their right and to their left all the
other ships were passing back and forth in peace and quiet. And the
ship that Jonah had boarded was in great difficulty and was about to
break up. They said, "On whose account has this evil befallen us?"

[So that] we will know on whose account this evil has befallen us
[we will cast lots] for the sake of [learning] who he is.

The sailors' confidence in the apparent random act of casting
lots seems absurd to us. It also bothered the commentators, and so
Abarbanel added an explanation: "They did not cast lots only once
because [if they had cast lots only one time the fact that it fell on
Jonah might have been the result of] random chance. Rather they
cast lots many times and they changed the lots, but each time the
lot fell on Jonah. And when they saw that despite the changes all the
attempts, [the result was the same], they believed that it was correct
[to conclude that the] result was from God and not a random event."

Malbim agrees with Abarbanel: "Why does [the text] say, 'They cast
lots,' in the plural? Should it not say, "They cast a lot" in the singular? The explanation [of why the text uses the plural *lots*] is that they
cast lots several times . . . and each time the lot fell on Jonah and
not on his shipmates." So both commentators consider the repeated
casting of lots as a reliable way of determining truth.

Abarbanel's explanation of the sailors' thinking supports the belief
in destiny and fate. Abarbanel writes, "Therefore their thoughts
agreed that the storm was because of the suffering of one of them.
Or perhaps the Eternal decreed, or [according to] the heavenly array
[the stars], a certain person [was destined] to die at that time in the
swirling waves of the storm. And if this was the case, it is proper
that the person would die at the appointed time. And thus the rest
of the people on the ship would not die with him."

While we think of fate as a Greek idea (recall the story of Oedi-
pus and how the Oracle at Delphi set his fate: that he would kill
his father and marry his mother), we do find threads of fate in the
Bible. The prophet Samuel, following God's direction, identifies the
very young David as the next king before David has done anything
to indicate that he deserves such an honor. Samuel's selection of
David surprises David's father and brothers. They see him as just a
little boy. David goes on to gain glory in individual combat and as a
military leader. He defeats Goliath, becomes Saul's leading general,

and when the time comes, he is in a position to follow Saul as king. He fulfills the destiny that Samuel proclaimed while he was still a boy. Moses' destiny as the leader of the people seems to be set at the moment of his birth. The events of his life inevitably lead him to stand at the burning bush and hear God's call.

How do we see our lives? Are our lives predestined? I hear people say, "Everything happens for a reason." Or "It's all part of God's plan." Once I heard a Chabad rabbi explain that life is like a tapestry, but we see it from the back and it appears to be random knots and strings. God sees it from the front and it is a beautiful work of art.

Years ago, a young man who had just completed his three years in the air force came to study for conversion with me. After he completed the process, he went to Israel to volunteer on a kibbutz for several months. During the time he was away, his mother suddenly took ill. He went to the airport in Israel to get on a flight as a stand-by passenger. The airline put him on a flight to Frankfurt. He missed the connection there, so he was sent to London to catch up with the flight. He again missed the connection. The flight he missed twice was Pan Am flight 109, which was blown up by terrorists over Scotland. The young man told me that his aunt said to him, "God saved you." He responded, "If I believe that, then I have to believe that God wanted everybody on the plane to die."

I can understand how some people find it comforting to believe in fate. We want life to make sense—that our lives are coherent narrative and not just disconnected random events. Seeing the hand of fate directing our lives provides that sense of coherence.

Our circumstances limit or enhance our choices. I grew up in a suburb of Minneapolis in the 1950s and 1960s. Because I was born in 1950 rather than in 1948, I escaped polio. Because of the efforts of my parents, I had the wide range of opportunities of the baby boom middle-class generation. My particular natural abilities limited and enhanced my opportunities. By the age of twelve, I knew it was not in my future to become a major league baseball player. I did not have the skills. When I was twenty-two, I did not have to decide if I wanted to be a rabbi or a cantor. I cannot carry a tune; I sing so poorly that I was the one told to just move my lips in the all-camp chorus.

Despite the appeal of thinking that we all have a destiny, and taking into consideration the benefits and barriers created by the specifics of our birth, I believe we own ourselves, that we make our own decisions and shape our own futures.

Alcoholism runs in families, but the child of an alcoholic does not have to live as an alcoholic. Adult children of divorced parents may be reluctant to wed because of the strife they witnessed as children, but they are not destined to have unhappy marriages. As Cassius reminds Brutus in Shakespeare's *Julius Caesar,* "The fault, dear Brutus, is not in our stars, but in ourselves."

My teacher, the late Rabbi Chanan Brichto, used to say that most people act as if everybody else has free will to do as they please but they themselves are forced to act as they do by circumstances beyond their control. Rabbi Brichto taught that we would be better off if we understood that everybody else is forced to act as they do by circumstances beyond their control but that we ourselves have free will to do as we please.

What We Really Know

Does Knowledge Lead to Virtue?

"Tell us, you who have brought this misfortune upon us?
What is your business? Where have you come from? What is
your country and of what people are you?" —JONAH 1:8

Why do the sailors pepper Jonah with these questions? Malbim sees the questions as those of primitive people. He writes:

"What is your business and so forth?" Because early people believed that there was a special master who was the god of the sea. And they foolishly believed that he had a hatred for a particular type of seafarers and would not allow them to cross the sea. And because of this they ask, "What is your business?" And they say that he has a hatred of particular places and he will not allow people of those places to enter the sea in peace. And therefore [the text says], "Where have you come from?" And he has a hatred of particular lands, that he hates the inhabitants and special nations. As is known of the foolishness of the early peoples, for this reason they ask, "What is your country and of what people are you?"

Malbim emphasizes the contrast between the sophisticated Jews, represented by Jonah, and less advanced nations of the world, represented by the sailors. He argues that the sailors still believe in multiple gods and magic, while Jonah is a believer in the One God of Israel and of reason.

Abarbanel takes a very different approach. He respects the sailors and explains, "The sailors do not immediately seize Jonah. And they do not [immediately] throw him into the sea because the lot fell on him. Rather they do an additional . . . investigation." They don't ask Jonah if he is the cause of the storm. They assume that to be true; the fact that the lot fell on Jonah convinces them that he is the cause of the storm. And now they want to understand what sin Jonah has committed to bring about such a calamity, so they ask him questions in order to learn the nature of his sin.

Kimchi explains that each of these questions identifies a specific area in Jonah's life in which he could have committed a sin that has brought about the storm. "What is your business? For what sin are you sought? What was your work? Perhaps it was the work of swindling and violence and because of this you are obligated [deserving punishment]. Where have you come from? Perhaps you fled from some evil you did there. What is your country? Perhaps the sons of that land are the sons of evil people."

Abarbanel offers another interpretation. "'What is your business?' . . . It means to say, 'Does that business [or ongoing regular activity] contain serious criminal behavior?' 'And where have you come from?' It means to say, 'Do you come from evil parents that the Holy One of Blessing visits their sins on you?' 'What is your country and of what people are you?' It means to say, 'Is your sin against the land, for example, disregarding sabbatical and jubilee years?' or 'Is your sin against your nation?'"

We see a stark difference between Malbim on one hand, who makes fun of the sailors, and Kimchi and Abarbanel on the other, who praise them for asking these questions.

From our twenty-first-century perspective, we see the sailors' confidence in the casting of lots as dubious, but we can praise their use of scientific inquiry. Like the sailors, we need to know why we do what we do. Simply following orders does not satisfy us. We want to participate in the decision-making process. It is natural for us is ask why.

The movement from the Age of Faith to the Age of Reason grew out of asking why. In the Age of Faith, one did not ask why, one believed. In the Age of Reason, asking why became central, for it fuels scientific inquiry. It motivated the European exploration of the rest of the world. The pursuit of knowledge stands as the central theme of western civilization.

The Jewish community has long praised the acquisition of knowledge. Jews give high priority to education and academic achievement. Many pursue knowledge-based careers in law, medicine, science, education, and academics. We take pride in the number of Jews who have been awarded Nobel Prizes.

Philosophers have linked knowledge with virtue since the time of Plato. But knowledge does not necessarily lead to virtue. The pursuit of virtue stands independent of the pursuit of knowledge. The sailors did not ask Jonah, "Where did you go to college? Where did you earn your PhD?" The sailors want to know, "With whom do you spend your time?"

Like the sailors, the sages in Pirke Avot stress the importance of the company we keep. "Yossei the son of Yoezer of Tzreidah would say: 'Let your home be a meeting place for the wise'" (Pirke Avot 1:4) and "Nitai the Arbelite would say: 'Distance yourself from a bad neighbor, do not cleave to a wicked person'" (Pirke Avot 1:7). These sages encourage us to spend time with the wise and shun the wicked in our midst.

We might not want to label the people we know as wicked. But if we refuse to recognize their misguided ways as wicked, we run the danger of getting entangled in their schemes.

A man I knew got caught up in corruption in the local court system. He explained to me that on his first day as a young prosecutor, one of the veteran members of the staff took him aside to explain to him how "things worked" at the courthouse. If he went along with the "system" that existed between the judges and the lawyers, he would receive a share of the bribes. He told me that he knew it was wrong and illegal, but he went along to get along. It was his first real job, and he wanted to be liked and to be successful. Ultimately a federal investigation unraveled the corrupt system, bringing charges against dozens of lawyers, judges, and court staff members. Almost all of them, including my friend, went to jail. He had not sought a life of crime, but he had allowed himself to be corrupted by those with whom he worked.

The sailors asked Jonah a series of questions to understand how he led his life. We too can ask ourselves questions: With whom do we spend our time? Do our friends, our relatives, and our co-workers draw us closer to a life of virtue?

12

I Am a Jew

How Do We Describe Our Identity?

"I am a Hebrew," he replied. —JONAH 1:9

In verse 8 the sailors ask Jonah many questions, but he does not always answer. Kimchi points out, "On two subjects he gives them answers. When he says to them, 'I am a Hebrew,' they know his people and his land."

Why does Jonah declare himself to be a Hebrew and not a Jew? Because in Jonah's time the term was not yet used to describe a member of the people.

If you ask twenty-first-century Jews who were the first Jews, they will quickly tell you Abraham and Sarah. But Abraham and Sarah would not have recognized the term *Jew*. It derives from the name of one of their grandsons, Judah, and the tribe that descended from him. The tribe of Judah was the dominant group in the Southern Kingdom during the First Temple period. Following the destruction of the Northern Kingdom and its ten tribes, the tribe of Judah becomes the dominant group in the nation. During the Second Temple period, the nation is called Judea. Late Hebrew Bible books use the term *Jew*. For example, "Now there was a Jew in the citadel of Susa whose name was Mordecai son of Jair son of Shimei son of Kish, a Benjaminite" (Esther 2:5). The first-century historian Josephus calls the people Jews, as does the author of the Gospel according to John.

It is interesting to note that later in history the term took on a pejorative meaning. Jewish organizations that were established in the United States in the nineteenth century do not have the term *Jewish* in their name. The preferred term in that era was *Hebrew*. There was the Washington Hebrew Congregation, founded in 1852; the

Indianapolis Hebrew Congregation, founded in 1856; the Hebrew Union College, founded in 1875; and Hebrew Immigrant Aid Society, founded in 1881.

In the context of the time and place in which he lived, it is natural for Jonah to define himself as a Hebrew. But the commentators look for deeper meaning in the term *Hebrew*. Ibn Ezra sees in the verse a description of Jonah's relationship to God. "He responds to them concerning the last [question]." Jonah tells them he is "a Hebrew, an Ivri." Ibn Ezra explains the source of the use of the Hebrew term *Ivri* to describe the Israelites. "He is from the sons of Iber who are called Ivri. For they follow the faith of the original Iber [monotheism]." Iber, sometimes spelled *Eber* in English, was a great-great-grandson of Noah. Ibn Ezra explains that Noah was the "ancestor of all the descendants of Iber" (Genesis 10:21). Genesis 11:16–26 lists the generations from Eber to Abraham, showing that Abraham, and hence all Israelites, are descendants of Eber, biologically and spiritually.

"He was in awe only of the Eternal from before whom he fled." Ibn Ezra explains that Jonah's flight should not be seen as a rejection of God's power. Nor did Jonah believe that God's power was limited to the Land of Israel. Ibn Ezra continues, "And he [Jonah, in the second half of this verse] proclaimed [that God formed] the heavens, the earth, and the sea and he reasons, 'For I know that He acts and will rule over it all.'" By declaring himself "Ivri," Jonah affirms his ongoing allegiance to the One God.

Abarbanel, seeking a more subtle meaning of this phrase, points out another possible meaning of these words. "I am a Hebrew, *Ivri anochi*": "There the intention of the text is not simply to indicate that he was from the land of the Hebrews but rather [it is a play on the word *Ivri* to mean that he] sinned." Out of the root *eiyin, vet, raish* one can form the word *Ivri*, Hebrew, and the word *aveira*, sin. "And he sinned against the commandment of his God." So when Jonah proclaims, "*Ivri anochi*," he says to the sailors, "I am a sinner," and he admits to God, "I am a sinner." No longer is he hiding his identity from the sailors or his location from God. With these two simple words, he identifies his nationality and moves on to the heart of the matter, his relationship to the Eternal.

The commentators see subtle meaning in Jonah's choice of words describing his identity. What meaning do we find in how we identify ourselves? I would say, "I am an American. I am a Jew. I am a Minnesotan living in Illinois. I am a Cubs fan." If someone says, "I am an Italian. My grandparents came to America from Italy. What are you?" I would respond, "I am a Jew."

My grandparents on one side and my great-grandparents on the other came to America from Lithuania. But I do not feel myself to be a Lithuanian. When my ancestors lived in Lithuania, the regular Lithuanians did not view my relatives as Lithuanians; they saw them as Jews who happened to be living in Lithuania. I do not speak Lithuanian. I do not even know a few words in Lithuanian to use when I get angry. I do not eat Lithuanian food, tell Lithuanian stories, or sing Lithuanian songs. I do not know much about Lithuanian history or Lithuanian national heroes. I do not own a Lithuanian flag; I do not even know the colors of the Lithuanian flag. I do not know the names of the current leaders of Lithuania, nor do I feel any special connection to the country.

But I do speak Hebrew. I eat Jewish food and sing Jewish songs. I know a great deal about Jewish history and Jewish national heroes. I feel a sense of kinship with Jews everywhere. In the old Soviet Union days, I worked to save Soviet Jewry. When the Jews of Ethiopia were in trouble, I joined the efforts to save them. I closely follow events in Israel. I read an Israeli newspaper every day, and I have been to Israel more than thirty times.

When I say, "I am a Jew," I am declaring my religion and my people. In the book of Ruth we read the famous conversation between Ruth and her mother-in-law, Naomi. Preparing to leave Moab and return to the Land of Israel, Naomi instructs her Moabite daughter-in-law to stay in Moab with her own parents. "Ruth replied, 'Do not urge me to leave you or to turn back and not follow you. Wherever you go

I will go; and wherever you lodge I will lodge; your people shall be my people and your God my God'" (Ruth 1:16). Ruth has become the model for people who choose to become Jews. Like Ruth they declare their commitment to the Jewish religion and to the Jewish people.

The meaning of terms changes over time. For example, before the Civil War the term *United States* was a plural. Prewar documents say the United States *are*. After the war *United States* became a singular: the United States *is*. This change has subtle but important significance, for it expresses the unity of our country. As Shelby Foote says in the documentary series *The Civil War*, this shift "sums up what the war accomplished. It made us an 'is.'"

The meaning of the declaration "I am a Jew" changes over time. There are moments in history and moments in our own individual lives when we emphasize the religious aspect and other times when we emphasize the peoplehood aspect. We each make the declaration in the context of the time and place realities of our lives.

Israeli author Yonatan Gefen in *Haish Hayarok* (The green man) tells the story of a green man who wakes up in a green morning, puts on his green clothes, and drives his green car. Everything in his world is green. Suddenly he sees a blue man. He asks the blue man, "What are you doing here?" The blue man responds, "I am from a different story."

As Jews in America we often feel we are from a different story. There is a fall day on which it is Yom Kippur for us and Wednesday for everybody else. There is a winter day on which for everybody else it is Christmas and for us it is Wednesday. Every three years I lead a Youth Israel Trip for the teens of my congregation during winter break. On those trips the kids marvel that in Israel December 25 is just an ordinary day.

As Jews in America we are from a different story. With how we lead our lives we express what it means to say, "I am a Jew."

13

Narrative Imagery

How Can We Understand Our Story?

"I worship the Eternal, the God of Heaven, who
made both the sea and the land." —JONAH 1:9

Why does this verse describe God as the one who made "the sea
and the land" rather than the more common biblical description of
God as the one who made "heaven and earth"? Dozens of times the
Hebrew Bible speaks of God as creator of heaven and earth, as in the
Creation story in Genesis and in Psalm 121:2: "My help comes from
the Eternal, maker of heaven and earth." When the Bible says, "God
that created the heaven and the earth," it expresses the extent of God's
power, that God created everything. Our Jonah text focuses on the
here and now of the story, the immediate context of the sailors' lives.

Kimchi explains, "Since they were engulfed by a storm at sea, he
said the God, Who is Blessed, made the sea. And He sent the storm
wind upon it. And He will quiet it when He will want to, and deliver
us to dry land." Kimchi points out that Jonah describes God's pow-
ers to the sailors from the situation that they all face.

Abarbanel adds that while Jonah has sinned against the Eternal
who rules over the heavens, the order in the heavens is not the problem that currently confronts Jonah and the sailors. Abarbanel writes,
"For it is the God of heaven whom I fear. And my sin is against Him.
But this matter does not depend on the order of the heavens. God,
who rules over them, has made the sea move and rage against us and
created the dry land to which we are unable to draw closer." The text
expresses God's power in the context of the narrative line of the story.

We can only appreciate a story or a reference if we understand its
context. In some biblical stories the texts provide the context that

the reader may not have understood. "And Abram moved his tent and came to dwell at the terebinths of Mamre, which are in Hebron, and he built an altar there to the Eternal" (Genesis 13:18). This verse explains that the unfamiliar location, the terebinths of Mamre, can be found near the well-known city of Hebron. The text presumes that the reader is familiar with Hebron but may not know the location of the terebinths of Mamre.

A few chapters later describing the location of the death of Sarah, the text says, "Sarah died at Kiriath Arba—now Hebron—in the land of Canaan" (Genesis 23:2). Again the author presumes that the reader knows the location of Hebron but might not know about the more obscure Kiriath Arba.

If we do not understand the details of a story we will lose track of its narrative line. Television programs often begin by saying, "Previously on . . ." And then we see key scenes from past episodes to establish the context for the new episode. In conversation we have to pay attention to the person with whom we are speaking when we use illustrations. I can count on my rabbi friends to "get" my references to Talmudic rabbis. I know my fellow Cubs fans will know that "the friendly confines" refers to Wrigley Field, the Cubs' stadium. But I cannot expect Cubs fans to know who Rabbi Tarphon was or my rabbi buddies to be able to identify Hack Wilson.

I spend a lot of time with teens at the synagogue, on Israel trips, and at summer camp. I am very careful in using youth culture references when teaching the teens. I have to be certain that I understand what I am talking about before I mention current music and movies. I do not want to be the guy who gets it wrong while trying too hard to relate to teenagers. In the opening song of Meredith Willson's musical *The Music Man*, the traveling salesmen sing, "But ya gotta know the territory." When we know the territory, we feel confident.

When we understand the context, we feel comfortable. When we do not understand the context, we feel like we are in a country where we do not speak the language. In an episode of *Star Trek: The Next Generation*, Captain Jean-Luc Picard of the starship *Enterprise* finds himself in a situation in which he cannot understand a thing being said to him despite his universal translator, which renders alien speech into English. He can hear the English words, but he doesn't get their context, and so they have no meaning for him.

In episode 102 Captain Picard is on a planet with a Tamarian starship captain. Rather than speaking in full sentences, the Tamarian utters phrases such as "Darmok and Jalad at Tanagra," "Temba, his arms wide," and "Shaka, when the walls fell." Eventually Picard figures out that the Tamarian's phrases refer to events in the mythic past of his people, and he is using them to express thoughts and feelings he wants to share through narrative imagery.

We also use narrative imagery when we refer to a movie, a song, or a TV show. We can quote phrases like "No soup for you!" (*Seinfeld*) or "Pay no attention to the man behind the curtain!" (*The Wizard of Oz*) without having to explain them. They convey full images. Edward Hall in his book *Beyond Culture* calls this kind of communication "high context." This shared cultural context creates a sense of community, and it helps us connect the dots of our own experiences.

Ship passengers who experience seasickness are often told to stare at the horizon to regain a sense of perspective and to calm themselves. They do not have the power to calm the lake or the sea, but they can try to calm themselves. We want to be able to connect the dots of our lives to form a meaningful picture. We cannot always control the circumstances of our lives, but if we understand the context of events, if we maintain our sense of horizon, we can calm ourselves so that we can survive the rough seas.

14

Fear and Awe

What Makes Us Tremble?

The men were greatly terrified, and they asked him,
"What have you done?" —JONAH 1:10

In Hebrew this verse opens "*Vayiru hanashim yirah gedola.*" A literal English translation is "The people feared a great fear." In English we wouldn't generally choose to use the same word in its verb and noun forms in the same sentence, but the Hebrew Bible often uses such sentence structure to express emphasis. A freer translation might be "They were greatly terrified." This phrase appears three times in the first chapter of the book of Jonah. We shall see that the meaning of the phrase shifts as the story moves along. What does it mean here in verse 10?

What do the sailors greatly fear? Here they seem to be afraid of God. Ibn Ezra explains: "In response to his [Jonah's] statement [in the previous verse, 'The Eternal, the God of heaven] I fear.' And they said to him, 'What is this? [What is your] reason [to fear]? How could you flee from before the Eternal?'" The sailors challenge Jonah: "You yourself proclaim the Eternal's power. How could you flee?"

Malbim suggests, "For what is written earlier [in verse 5 is] that 'the sailors feared.' This was a fear of danger [of the ship breaking apart in the storm]. But here [in verse 10] this fear is the fear of the Eternal that is great and uplifting according to the greatness of the strength that He permits to flow from Him."

Abarbanel focuses on the second half of the verse. "In their realization of the cause of their great difficulty in this voyage they asked Jonah another [question]. 'What have you done?' It is not their only question. Rather it is an expression as if to say, 'How could you do such a thing to rebel against the word of the Eternal, to flee from before Him?' And it will be [expressed here as] 'What have you done?'"

Malbim agrees with Abarbanel: "I want to say, 'How could you have done such an evil thing to flee from the presence of the Eternal? Do you not fear Him?'"

Should we be surprised that fear moves Jonah to flee? Or that fear moves the sailors to take drastic action to save the ship? How do we respond to fear? How do we react when we feel threatened? Walter Cannon describes animal response in his book *Wisdom of the Body*: "The fight-or-flight response is a physiological reaction that occurs in response to a perceived harmful event, attack, or threat to survival." Like animals we can stand our ground and fight—or we can flee, seeking safety.

History provides us with innumerable examples of those who stood firm against overwhelming odds. Just about every American child knows the story of Davy Crockett at the Alamo. This legendary frontiersman and 130 others chose to stand and fight rather than flee, and they defended the Alamo against 1,000 Mexican soldiers for thirteen days. "Remember the Alamo!" became the rallying cry for the other Texas forces in their defeating the Mexicans at the decisive Battle of San Jacinto two months later.

We lead lives that are significantly less dramatic than Davy Crockett's, but we do face fear, fear that at times overwhelms us. How do we move forward?

Perhaps the best known advice Americans ever got about confronting fear was from Franklin Delano Roosevelt in his Inaugural Address on March 4, 1933. At the depth of the Depression, President Roosevelt declared, "So, first of all, let me assert my firm belief that the only thing we have to fear is fear itself—nameless, unreasoning, unjustified terror which paralyzes needed efforts to convert retreat into advance." Roosevelt understood that fear prevented the country from acting together to fight its way out of the Depression. Americans' fear of the further collapse of their lives paralyzed them. He called upon the nation to take bold action, and during FDR's first hundred days in office his administration moved fifteen major bills through Congress including legislation that reopened the nation's shuttered banks.

Most everyone familiar with the Bible knows the 23rd Psalm and its verse 4: "Yea, though I walk through the valley of the shadow of death, I will fear no evil: For Thou art with me." The speaker expresses confidence despite the threat of evil and death. This confidence comes from the knowledge that God is present. We proclaim that we are not alone in the universe, that there is more to existence than what we know in this material world.

In a classic comedy bit, in the book *The 2000-Year-Old Man in the Year 2000*, Carl Reiner asks the 2,000-Year-Old Man, played by Mel Brooks, about God. "We believed in a superior being. His name was Phil. Phil was big and strong. . . . Nobody was as powerful as Phil. If he wanted, he could kill you. As a result, we revered him and prayed to him. . . . 'Oooh, Philip, please don't hurt us! . . . Philip, please don't pinch us!' But one day Phil was hit by a bolt of lightning. All of a sudden we looked up at the sky and said, 'There's something bigger than Phil!'" In later chapters there will be more refined understandings of God, but for now, "There's something bigger than Phil!" works.

Most often English versions of the Bible translate *yirah* as fear, but it can also be translated as awe. When Jacob wakes up from his dream, he declares, "How awesome is this place, *Ma morah hamakom hazeh*" (Genesis 28:17). Jacob feels awe, not fear. We call the High Holidays the Days of Awe, not the Days of Fear (*Yamim Noraim*, in which *Norah* shares the three-letter root with the word *yira*).

Later in the book of Jonah, after the sailors throw Jonah into the sea, the storm quiets and the sailors realize that they are saved. The text uses the same phrase it uses here in verse 10 to describe the sailors' response in verse 16. "The men feared the Eternal greatly" (1:16). Here we can read *yira* to mean awe rather than fear and translate this as "Then they were greatly in awe of the Eternal." Earlier fear fills the hearts of the sailors, but by verse 16 they no longer fear the destruction of their ship; they now stand in awe before the One God.

What is the connection between fear and awe? They both describe an experience of being overwhelmed by that which is great and powerful. Fear is our response to a threatening other. We fear that our lives are spinning out of control. We fear that the structure that has held our lives together has collapsed. Awe is our response to a more beneficent other. The overwhelming challenges that confronted us have been resolved. The source of order in the universe has brought order to our lives. The emotional state of the sailors moves from fear to awe, as their situation shifts from chaos to resolution. As we walk the paths of our lives, we hope to mirror this progress from chaos to resolution, from fear to awe.

15

Troubled Waters

How Can We Calm the Sea?

"What must we do to you to make the sea calm around us?" For
the sea was growing more and more stormy. —JONAH I:II

Like the sailors, we encounter unexpected storms in our lives. What
can we do when we hit a stormy situation in our lives? The sailors
turn to Jonah for direction.

The sailors don't ask, "What should we do?" They ask, "What
should we do *to you*?" Ibn Ezra writes, "And the reason [that the
sailors ask Jonah], 'What should we do to you?' is because they want
direction from the person who understands the ways of the Eternal.
[They say,] 'Give us advice as to what to do.'"

Here, as he often does, Kimchi provides a voice-over, explaining
the thought process of the characters. He imagines the sailors thinking, "For we have no hope that the sea will become quiet without
God's intervention because the storm increases in ferocity."

The sailors are really asking Jonah for guidance. What can they do
to persuade God to quiet the sea in this "place of its strong waves"?
Kimchi refers to the 107th Psalm, which speaks of "Others who go
down to the sea in ships . . . they have seen the works of the Eternal
and His wonders in the deep." It describes a storm with huge waves.
The sailors caught in that storm cry out to God, who responds to
their prayer. "He reduced the storm to a whisper, and the waves were
stilled. They rejoiced when all was quiet."

While the sailors may speak of their own efforts to please God,
they do realize that since Jonah created the difficulty by fleeing from
God, he will have to act to resolve the situation. Abarbanel also
explores the sailors' thinking: "And here the sailors with all the lots

they cast time after time indicating the guilt of Jonah, like a hundred witnesses, still they did not throw him into the sea. [Rather] they asked him, 'What must we do to make the sea calm around us?' It means to say that after you fled from before the Blessed One, how can you repair this?" Abarbanel imagines the sailors contemplating three possible questions:

1. Should we go to the place about which the King, God, spoke and cause His thoughts to be brought there? The sailors suggest that they could fulfill Jonah's mission by going to Nineveh themselves.
2. Or you will swear an oath to the Eternal, an oath to the Protector of Jacob, to go there and fulfill his commandment.
3. Or is there another way to become obedient to God's will, in order to cleanse you of your sin?

Malbim imagines the sailors considering two possible methods of sending Jonah on his way to Nineveh: "They asked him if he wanted to turn in repentance to accept upon himself [the mission] to go to Nineveh. Perhaps they will have [the opportunity] to remedy [the situation by their hands] that they will repent with him and travel to the harbor that leads to Nineveh or they will return him to the Land of Israel [from which he would travel to Nineveh]. And as a result it will 'make the sea calm around us.'"

We all encounter stormy weather in our day-to-day lives. As the sailors consider various ways to calm the seas around themselves, we look to make the sea calm around us.

In my work as a congregational rabbi I often find myself trying "to make the sea calm." Early in my career I was helping a bar mitzvah boy prepare for his big day. His recently divorced parents were not speaking to one another. To arrange the honors for the service, I engaged in shuttle diplomacy speaking first to one parent and then to the other. After many conversations I negotiated a deal on the honors. Both parents accepted an "equitable" division of the parts in the service between the members of both halves of the family. I was proud of my diplomatic accomplishment. On the morning of the bar mitzvah, the father walked out of the synagogue because his son would not say hello to him.

I was young, inexperienced, and filled with confidence in my ability to shape events to fit my vision. Now I understand that I cannot solve the conflict between two people with my clever ideas. I can only encourage them to resolve their own problems.

I also understand that calming the waters is not the same as solving the underlying problem. Often the problem is complex, involving too much history and bitterness to be quickly resolved. But I can calm the immediate situation. Sometimes I can do so with my tone of voice. I can switch from my regular loud, energetic voice to speaking like Fred Rogers.

When my children were young I was not a big fan of *Mr. Rogers' Neighborhood*. But I have come to understand that speaking slowly and quietly can "soothe a savage breast" (William Congreve) or calm the aggravated teenager. Also we can keep the waters calm by avoiding being drawn into unnecessary conflicts. People try to bait us. They say things to get a rise out of us. We do not have to take the bait. We can recognize the bait as bait and ignore it. We do not have to mistake the bait for food. When people speak to us in anger, attacking us for something we said or did, their emotional intensity tempts us to respond with equal intensity. But we do not have to act that way. We can take the judo approach. Rather than trying to stand strong to absorb the blow, we can step out of the way and let their energy carry them past us. Rather than responding with anger of our own, we can say something bland and flat like "That's interesting." Our calm demeanor and soft spoken response can calm the waters.

Our role model should be Hillel. One day someone wagered that he could make Hillel angry. The bet was 400 pieces of gold. It was just before Shabbat, and Hillel the Elder was preparing for its arrival. The man therefore rushed to Hillel's home and cried, "Hillel the Elder! Where's Hillel the Elder?"

At the time Hillel was washing himself, and so he interrupted his preparations, wrapped himself in his clothes, and went to the one who was calling him. "What do you want, my son?" he asked.

"I have a question to ask you."

"Ask me then."

"Why are the heads of Babylonians so round?"

And Hillel the Elder, himself Babylonian, answered him with a smile. "You have asked a profound question, my son, and I will answer you. It is because they have bad midwives that don't know how, when a baby is born, to give the head a good shape."

The man didn't reply. Later, he asked Hillel: "Why are the people of Tadmor weak-eyed?"

"Because they live in a sandy country," Hillel the Elder replied.

After a certain time, the man came back and asked, "Why do Africans have such wide feet?"

With inexhaustible patience, Hillel the Elder answered: "Because they live in a marshy land."

"I still have many questions to ask you," said the man, "but I am afraid of making you angry."

"Ask on, my son," said Hillel the Elder. "Ask me everything you want to know."

Although Shabbat was arriving, Hillel the Elder sat down in order to be more attentive to the unusual questions that this stranger wanted to ask.

"Are you really Hillel," said the man, "whom they call a prince in Israel?"

"Yes, that is correct, my son," he replied.

"Well, I hope that here are not many more in Israel like you!"

"And why not, my son?" asked Hillel.

"Because of you," said the man, "I have lost 400 pieces of gold, for I wagered that I could make you angry."

"Be warned for the future," said Hillel the Elder. "Better that you should lose 400 pieces of gold, and 400 more after that, than it should be said of Hillel that he lost his temper!" (TB Shabbat 31a)

We may not see an obvious or immediate solution to the problems that we or those around us face, but there is no need to panic now. We can climb out on the ledge later. There are always alternatives to consider, choices to make. Sometimes circumstances profoundly limit our choices. But we can impact the circumstances. We can calm the waters by the way we speak and act.

16

The Winning Team

What Do We Need from Other People?

He answered them, "Heave me overboard and the sea
will calm down for you, for I know that this terrible storm
came upon you on my account." —JONAH 1:12

Most of us depend on the people around us every day for one thing or another. Our friends, our relatives, and our co-workers contribute to the quality and ease of our lives. Jonah seeks unusual help from the sailors. He asks them to throw him into the sea to drown. Jonah believes that this is the only way that the sailors can save themselves.

In the previous chapter we read commentary on the sailors' different ideas of how the mission to Nineveh could be completed. Here in verse 12, Jonah takes another approach. As Ibn Ezra explains, Judah asked to die. Jonah does not speak of repenting of his sin and seeking to resume his life as a prophet. Rather he prefers death so that he will not be required to draw the Ninevites back to the Eternal. As Ibn Ezra explained in his comment to verse 1, Jonah wanted to protect the honor of Israel. He feared that if he prophesied to the Ninevites, they would repent of their sins, thereby bringing shame upon the Israelites who never repent of their sins in response to the call of the prophets. Jonah would rather give up his own life than bring shame upon Israel. "And he did not say this to them [the sailors], so that he would not hear from their mouths that they would send him [to Nineveh]." Jonah was concerned that if he explained to the sailors the entire situation, they would not seek to quiet the sea by killing him, but rather by sending him on his mission to Nineveh.

Abarbanel explains the meaning of Jonah's rejection of the sailors' suggestions for resuming his mission:

He means to say, "I do not want to go to Nineveh. I do not choose to turn in repentance or to swear an oath to go there, to fulfill The Blessed One's mission. For it seems good to me that you will throw me into the sea and I will die there. From that which appears to you to do to save yourselves, do not cease again. For I know that this great storm is upon you because of me." And here Jonah ceases his repentance and chooses to stifle his soul and die in the depths of the sea so that he will not go to save the Assyrians who in the future will be aroused by God to cause the death of the Northern Kingdom of Israel and destroy it. And thus is the case his intention was to serve heaven.

Abarbanel argues that Jonah did not flee out of selfish fear. Rather, his flight was motivated by concern for the future of the Northern Kingdom. If he did not go to Nineveh, the capital of the Assyrian Empire, the Ninevites would not repent. If they did not repent, God could not use them as the rod of Divine anger to destroy the Northern Kingdom. Therefore Jonah flees. He remains committed to the larger goal: saving the Northern Kingdom. Abarbanel presents Jonah as a heroic figure prepared to sacrifice himself to save his people.

Kimchi explains that Jonah explicitly connects the storm with his sin. When Jonah says, "On my account," he means to say, "Because of the sin that is mine."

Malbim continues this line of interpretation, putting in words Jonah's thoughts: "And this I know clearly. The storm is not for you as a punishment for you for what you have done by bringing me to Tarshish, for this is not the way the Eternal works. Only I know that this terrible storm came upon you on my account to punish me alone, not because of you. When I sink into the sea, the sea will become quiet around you."

Jonah courageously tells the sailors to throw him overboard. He believes this will lead to his death and the survival of the sailors. But why do the sailors have to throw him into the sea? Why can't he jump into the sea himself? Why does he require sailor-assisted suicide?

It is generally understood that our religious tradition opposes suicide. But two other biblical figures do take their own lives: King Saul and Samson. Jonah does not have the strength of will of Saul or Samson. Jonah plays a more passive role. He has concluded that he must die for the sailors to live, but he depends upon them to kill him.

While Jonah thought he had to depend on others to "die," we depend on others to live. Depending on others does not lessen our value; rather, it increases the richness of our lives.

In the 1952 movie *The Winning Team,* Ronald Reagan plays baseball legend Grover Cleveland Alexander. Doris Day plays his wife, Aimee. The film is every bit as hokey as the cast suggests. Critics argue that it offers a romanticized telling of Alexander's life, playing fast and loose with the historic details. Nonetheless, I love this movie.

Alexander was one of the best pitchers in Major League baseball in the decade before America entered World War I. While serving in the war Alexander was gassed and suffered shell shock, which causes the onset of physical problems. When he returned home from the war, he self-medicated with alcohol. In the film, Aimee remains loyal to him and convinces Rogers Hornsby, the manager of the St. Louis Cardinals, to give her husband a chance to resurrect his career.

During the 1926 season Alexander leads the Cardinals to the World Series. Aimee is always in the stands. Whenever Alexander begins to feel dizzy and weak on the mound, he looks at Aimee in the stands and regains his strength.

As the season nears conclusion, Alexander says to Aimee: "You must be so tired, dear."

"Why should I be tired?"

"I've been stealing strength from you all season—every game, every pitch. Without you there, I couldn't have done any of it."

In the World Series Alexander pitches complete game victories in games 2 and 6. Aimee does not attend the decisive seventh game because there is no way that Hornsby could use Alexander after he had pitched a complete game the day before.

In the seventh inning with the bases loaded and the Cardinals leading 3–2, Hornsby turns to Alexander to face Yankee star Tony Lazzeri. In the film Aimee comes out of her Times Square hotel and sees on the electronic reader board the news that her husband is being called upon to pitch. She jumps in a cab and says to the driver, "Get me to the Yankee Stadium." A police car provides an escort.

While warming up, Alexander has difficulty. He looks into the stands searching for Aimee. She is not there. Then at the last second she arrives. Alexander regains his strength and confidence. He strikes out Lazzeri. He goes on to pitch the final two innings without giving up a run. The Cardinals win the series. The Cardinals are the "Winning Team." Grover and Aimee are the "Winning Team."

We too can be part of a winning team, but we need teammates. We cannot go it alone. We need to be in a relationship with others, people we can depend upon to be present for us as Aimee was present for Grover. She does not give up on him even when he behaves in a self-destructive manner. She battles on his behalf. And at a key moment she is there for him, literally and metaphorically.

Jonah needs the sailors, and the sailors need Jonah. We need family, friends, and community. We need to be able to look into the eyes of another person and know that they care for us, as we care for them.

17

The Giants Win the Pennant

*How Can We Differentiate between the
Possible and the Impossible?*

> Nevertheless the men rowed hard to regain the shore,
> but they could not, because the sea was growing more
> and more stormy about them. —JONAH 1:13

The sailors ask Jonah: "What must we do to make the sea calm around us?" (Jonah 1:11). Jonah tells them that they should throw him into the sea. But they aren't willing to comply. They cannot yet accept the truth that Jonah has shared with them—that the only way to save their lives is to take his life. They don't want to take Jonah's life; they don't want his blood on their hands. They believe that they can use their skills as sailors to overcome the storm and save Jonah. Abarbanel explains:

> And when the sailors had heard the words of Jonah, his question and his request, they did not obey his instruction [to throw him into the sea]. Instead, they rowed and exerted themselves "to regain the shore" in order to remove Jonah from the ship and send him on his mission to quickly deliver the injunction in Nineveh. And The Holy One did not choose this path for Jonah for He wanted Jonah of his own free will to repent and ask to go where the Holy One had sent him. And they were not able to reach the shore because the sea stormed around them and the wind came from the land. And it held the ship in such a way that it was not able to draw closer to the land.

No matter how hard they tried, the sailors' skills could not overcome the circumstances created by God.

Malbim calls our attention to the sailors' motivation: "If the main intention of the Eternal was to return him to his land from which he had fled, would it not appear reasonable to the sailors that they would be able to return to dry land to bring the fugitive back to his master? But they could not, because the sea was growing more and more stormy about them. After Jonah did not turn in repentance, the storm did not rise to silence." Despite Jonah's refusal to repent, and his refusal to pledge to go to Nineveh, nevertheless, the sailors row hard, trying to bring the ship back to dry land. They imagine that they can reach the land and send Jonah on his way to Nineveh.

In Malbim's interpretation, the sailors see themselves as helping God's plan along by attempting to bring Jonah back against his will. They try once more to overcome the storm through conventional means, rather than quickly throwing Jonah into the sea. But they do not realize that they cannot resist God's plan.

While other Hebrew words could have been used, *vayacht'ru* is a more poetic way of describing the intensity of the sailors' actions. Ibn Ezra explains, "And the word *vayacht'ru* [which generally means digging] is used because the rowers are similar to diggers." As diggers place their shovels in the soil and pull, so oarsmen place their oars in the water and pull. They fully throw themselves into their work, believing that through the strength of their effort they will be able to save Jonah.

Jonah has explained the situation to the sailors and has told them what they must do, but they do not want to accept the fact that Jonah must die for them to be saved. They refuse to accept the harsh reality before them.

It is human nature to refuse to give up. Often we praise the person who remains committed to a goal no matter what the odds. Every four years during the television coverage of the Olympics, we see human-interest stories showing us the efforts of the athlete preparing for the competition. We see the skier or the skater, the swimmer or the gymnast rising before daybreak to begin their strenuous daily workout routine. We see how their deep, unwavering commitment has enabled them to stand with the world's best athletes. We admire this commitment to persist. But sometimes, like the sailors rowing to reach the shore, we find ourselves engaged in efforts that cannot succeed. At these moments we need the wisdom to choose another path.

Too many times I have visited people who have just received the awful news that they have an incurable disease. Sometimes they or their family will not accept this diagnosis and they devote themselves to searching for the nonexistent "new" treatment. They row hard to regain the shore. But like the sailors in our story, their goal is unreachable.

When my father's pancreatic cancer was discovered, it was too far along for effective treatment. I started hearing from friends that they were praying for my father's recovery. As a result of my interfaith work, I have lots of friends in religious communities. Orders of nuns were praying for my father; Catholic monks were praying for my father; Evangelical Christians were praying for my father. Muslims, Baha'i, and Zoroastrians and Jews in different synagogues were praying for my father. I felt supported by these prayers; I knew I was not alone. But I understood that no amount of prayer could stop this cancer. The question was not how to save my father's life but what to do during the months he had left. I live in Chicago. My parents were in California. He was diagnosed in December, and shortly thereafter I went to see him. I was thinking about going back in March for another visit, but then I had a better idea.

My father and I both loved baseball. He was a lifelong Giants fan. He grew up in Manhattan, and as a child he went to see the New York Giants at the Polo Grounds. When we were growing up in Minnesota, we heard stories of Mel Ott's home runs and Carl Hubbell's screwball. My brother and I were among the few boys in Minnesota in the early sixties who could duplicate Mel Ott's unusual batting stance. We knew that Carl Hubbell struck out five future Hall of Famers in a row in the 1934 All-Star Game: Babe Ruth, Lou Gehrig, Jimmie Foxx, Al Simmons, and Joe Cronin.

And, of course, my father's favorite baseball story was of Bobby Thomson's home run to win the 1951 playoff series for the Giants over their archenemies, the Brooklyn Dodgers. Nowadays one can easily pull up a clip of this moment on the Internet. When we were kids, our father had a phonograph record of the announcer Russ Hodges's call of that moment: "The Giants win the pennant, the Giants win the pennant, the Giants win the pennant, the Giants win the pennant."

Living in the Bay Area my father again was able to root in person for his Giants. That winter I suggested to my father that if he was up to it, he should meet me in Arizona in March for spring training. It worked. We spent a few days together in Arizona. Each afternoon we went to a ballgame, and in the mornings and evenings we talked. It was the only trip that my father and I ever took, just the two of us. My father died early that July. Suggesting this trip to spring training was the best idea I ever had.

No amount of rowing could bring our ship closer to the shore. But because I had figured out what was possible and what wasn't for my father then, we were able to make the most of the moments we had together. My father died more than twenty years ago, but still when I watch a show of the greatest moments in baseball history, there is always one clip that makes me cry.

18

The Buck Stops Here

Can We Accept Responsibility?

> "O Eternal, please do not let us perish on account of this man's
> life. Do not hold us guilty of killing an innocent person! For You,
> Eternal, by Your will, You have brought this about." —JONAH 1:14

Having seen that their efforts to row to shore could not succeed, the
sailors pause to pray before they throw Jonah into the sea. Rashi
looks closely at the wording of the phrase, "Do not hold us guilty of
killing an innocent person," *b'nefesh haish hazeh*. It means "In this
man's soul." Rashi understands the *bet* at the beginning of *"b'nefesh"*
to mean "on account of." The sailors ask the God of Israel not to
punish them on account of what they are about to do to Jonah.
Rashi imagines them saying, "[We do not want to suffer] for the sin
of endangering his life with our own hands." The sailors take that
act of throwing Jonah into the sea seriously. They understand it to
be the taking of his life. They want to be sure that everyone understands it as a fulfillment of God's wishes and not an act of violence.

Ibn Ezra provides support for Rashi's understanding of the *bet*
at the beginning of *b'nesfesh*. "This [unusual usage of the preposition *bet*] is similar to 'And Jacob served [seven years] on account of
Rachel *(b'Rachel)'"* (Genesis 29:20). In both cases the preposition
bet is understood not as meaning "in" but rather "for."

The text tells us that they cried, "O Eternal." The text uses the
four-letter name of God, Yud Hey Vav Hey, to describe the target of
their prayers. Earlier, in verse 5, each sailor prayed to his own god.
Here the sailors pray to the one God of Israel, acknowledging the
power of that God. Their use of the four-letter name of the Eternal
in their prayer demonstrates that they have come to understand

that YHVH truly rules the universe. As Ibn Ezra explains, "They all believed in the Eternal One of Glory." Because of their experience with Jonah and the storm, they have become believers in the Eternal One of Glory. Ibn Ezra continues, "And they turned to Him to call upon [Him in prayer]."

Ibn Ezra explains the meaning of the last phrase of this verse, "as You wished." "[This is an expression] that it was clear to them [the sailors] that on his [Jonah's] account the sea was storming." They recognize that the storm was not a normal natural occurrence, but rather an act of God in response to Jonah's flight. Before they throw Jonah into the sea, they proclaim out loud that they do this only in response to God's will.

Abarbanel clarifies the sailors' position. They want to be understood as following God's wishes, but it is not God's will for them to die along with Jonah, who is the target of Divine anger.

> There is no escaping from this decision whether this man is designated to die for his sin or not. And if he is designated to die for his sin, this one man will sin. And toward the entire company of the ship do not become angry. Do not let us be destroyed for the soul of this man. For his sinful soul will die in this way or in a plague or in some other manner. For there is no stopping the hand of the Eternal from striking His enemy and the myriads who curse the Eternal. And why should we be destroyed because of him? And if he is not designated to die, "Do not place on us innocent blood," in that we have sent him into the sea and have killed him and shed his blood for no reason. And do not say that You have no other way to kill him except by destroying the ship he is on. For You are the Eternal, for what You want, You do. And always when You proclaim, it is not an empty saying. And many openings exist to fulfill the Divine will [of destroying Jonah] without destroying us.

Malbim continues Abarbanel's reasoning: "They want to say that if we had not thrown him into the sea, would we not have been destroyed because of the soul of this man? That on account of his sinful soul we would all be lost. And that is not what we deserve. And if we throw him into the sea, on this side we ask, Do not count it as 'innocent blood,' to punish us for his drowning."

In Malbim's explanation of the last phrase of the verse he completes the argument. Jonah's blood is on God's hands, not the sailors': "For You, Eternal, by Your will, You have brought this about." Malbim writes, "They [the sailors] want to say to [God] that this act [of causing Jonah's death by throwing him into the sea] is not connected with us but only with You, for You brought this storm and You wanted to drown him in the sea and You did as [You wished.] For we are forced to do this, for if we do not throw him into the sea we will all drown. Therefore this deed is connected to You and not to us."

The sailors' position, renouncing responsibility, reminds me of two later events. In the Christian Bible. In Matthew 27:22–25, Pontius Pilate speaks to the people of Jerusalem: "What shall I do, then, with Jesus who is called the Messiah?" Pilate asked. They all answered, "Crucify him!" "Why? What crime has he committed?" asked Pilate. But they shouted all the louder, "Crucify him!" So when Pilate saw that he was gaining nothing, but rather that a riot was beginning, he took water and washed his hands before the crowd, saying, "I am innocent of this man's blood; see to it yourselves." All the people answered, "His blood is on us and on our children!"

In the Jonah text the sailors absolve themselves of responsibility and place all the responsibility in God's hands. In the Matthew text, the author has Pilate absolving himself of responsibility for the coming execution of Jesus and placing the responsibility in the hands of the people.

In 1921 Lt. Karl Neumann, a U-boat captain responsible for the sinking of a British hospital ship, the *Dover Castle*, during World War I, stood trial in Germany. He was acquitted from criminal liability on the grounds that he was under superior orders to sink the ship.

Legal scholar George A. Finch commented that "all civilized nations recognize the principle that a subordinate is covered by the orders of his superiors" (Superior Orders and War Crimes, July 1921).

The Allies addressed this same issue in advance of the Nuremberg Trials after World War II. The protocols for the Nuremberg Trials state, "The fact that a person acted pursuant to order of his Government or of a superior does not relieve him from responsibility under international law, provided a moral choice was in fact possible to him."

In our day we have witnessed countless acts of violence performed "in the name of God." While it is easy for Jews to point out examples from other religious communities, Jews too have killed in the name of God. On Purim in 1994 Dr. Baruch Goldstein entered the mosque at the Cave of the Patriarchs in Hebron and opened fire, killing twenty-nine Muslims.

In our day people continue to claim, "I was only following orders." We can find examples in military settings, in the business world, and in government. The sailors in our story do not want to accept responsibility for what they are about to do to Jonah. They pass the buck to God.

A wooden sign describing the need to accept responsibility sat on President Harry Truman's desk in the White House. He explained:

> You know, it's easy for the Monday morning quarterback to say what the coach should have done after the game is over. But when the decision is up before you—and on my desk I have a motto which says, "The Buck Stops Here"—the decision has to be made.
>
> When my government acts, a portion of the responsibility of the action falls on me. I have a moral imperative to participate in the forming of the policies of my government. I cannot absent myself from the realm of politics, even though it may be frustrating. I cannot dismiss involvement in government by saying, "They are all crooks." They act as my agents. It is my task to raise my voice,

insisting on "clean hands and pure hearts" (Psalm 24:4). We cannot blame our actions on any others, divine or human. We need to follow a course of responsibility: I am responsible for everything I do and I share in the responsibility of everything done on my behalf. (National War College, December 19, 1952)

19

The Scientific Method

How Can We Solve Our Problems One Step at a Time?

And they heaved Jonah overboard, and the
sea stopped raging. —JONAH 1:15

Newton's Third Law of Motion proclaims, "For every action, there is an equal and opposite reaction." The sea quiets immediately after Jonah is thrown overboard. The Bible sees Jonah's entering the sea as causing the storm to stop. It is the reaction to the sailors' action.

Abarbanel draws our attention to exactly how the sailors threw Jonah into the sea:

And after all these efforts when the sailors saw that in every way the sea continued to storm about them, they lowered Jonah into the sea. And in truth these words teach that they tried to save him. . . . And this follows what is said in Pirke de Rebbi Eliezer (chapter 10) "They lowered him into the sea up to his knees and the sea quieted from its raging. They returned him [to the ship] pulling him up to them. Immediately the sea began to storm. They again lowered him into the sea, [this time] up to his neck, and the sea quieted from its raging. They returned him to the ship pulling him up to them. Immediately the sea began to storm until they lowered him entirely into the sea." They did these many experiments to know for certain that the reason [for the storm] was Jonah. And the sages, may their memory be for a blessing, [came to this understanding] in their precise reading of the words of the text. For it literally says, "Pick me up and throw me [sa'uni vahatiluni]" (Jonah 1:12). [The rabbis build off Jonah's use of two Hebrew words rather than one word. Why didn't Jonah simply say, "Throw me"?] This teaches that they performed two discrete actions. They lowered him into the sea and drew him out of there to see the truth of the matter. And this explains what is said [in this verse literally]: "They lifted up Jonah and lowered him into the sea." After they withdrew him from the sea several times, finally they lowered him into the sea to stay.

The sailors' experiment of throwing Jonah into the sea yields the same result all three times. And so they conclude that throwing Jonah into the sea will indeed quiet the waters. They now feel certain that God wants them to act.

Malbim ties this last experiment to the other steps in the sailors' process of discovering the truth about Jonah:

> At the beginning they carried him in their hands and they performed several trials and they saw that when they lowered him the sea stood quietly from its anger. And it is the case that they would not have lowered him into the water without certainty [that the storm was because of him], for they had many tests: the unique character of the storm that it only affected this ship, from the many castings of the lots which all fell on Jonah, from his own announcement, and from the final experience that each time that they lowered him into the sea it stood [quiet] from its storming.

The sailors do not rush to judgment, they do not rely on the casting of the lots, nor do they take Jonah at his word when he tells them what they have to do. They attempt a less drastic approach—they try to row to shore. And even when they begin to accept the fact that they need to cast Jonah into the sea to save the ship and themselves, they proceed slowly.

I find that too often communities move too fast in trying to solve a problem. They begin to talk about solutions before they have clearly defined the problem. Somebody I know well recently consulted with me about how to present to the board a plan to restructure the congregation's staff. I suggested a two-step presentation. She should first present the need for a change, providing the board members the opportunity to discuss the need. Only after the board agrees a need exists should she present the plan. If she had made a single-step presentation, those wishing to raise questions about the need and those raising questions about the plan would be jumbled together. It makes for a more confusing conversation. And it builds opposition rather than support. People who accepted the needs but disagreed with the specifics of the plan would meld together with those who rejected the idea that change was needed, to form a negative chorus.

In our individual lives we tend to layer the problems we face, one on top of the other, rather than sorting them out and dealing with one at a time. By layering the problems we add to the weight we feel on our shoulders. We feel overburdened. This accumulated weight bends us over so we do not feel we have strength to do anything. Some days we feel like we are confronting the "slings and arrows of outrageous fortune" (Shakespeare). And at times that is truly the case. We face catastrophic illness or the death of a loved one. But at other times our sense of "the slings and arrows" grows out of combining what should be seen as separate problems.

It's best to take the problems off our shoulders and sort them out. We can arrange them by topic: health, finances, family. Or we can rank them serious to trivial. Or we might lay them out by solutions: these problems I can solve on my own, but for these problems I will need help. We can produce a map of our problems. Sylvia Johnson, in her book *Mapping the World*, writes:

> Maps show us how to get from one place to another, but they have other stories to tell. By looking at a map, we can see which aspects of the world were most important to people in a particular time and place. The earliest maps from ancient Mesopotamia picture a small world made up only of neighboring kingdoms. During the Middle Ages, when Christianity was a powerful influence, maps often showed the location of the Garden of Eden and other places mentioned in the Bible. In a later period of trade and exploration,

mapmakers produced sea charts based on compass readings to guide sailors as they navigated unknown seas. With the discovery of new lands and new peoples, the known world was transformed, and maps reveal the different stages of this great change.

At this point in the Jonah story the sailors have learned a great deal about Jonah. When they first met him in verse 3 they saw him simply as another passenger. Now they have a more comprehensive "map" of Jonah's life and character. From their experiences, they understand that Jonah's flight from God has caused the storm that threatens their lives.

Mapping our problems can serve as an important first step in solving them. With a fully defined map of the challenges we face, we can begin to plot a course with the goal of solving the problems one at a time. We can choose which ones to confront now and which ones to avoid for the time being. Maps of shopping centers often include a "you are here" arrow to orient the shoppers to the locations of the stores they seek. Mapping our problems can provide us with a similar sense of understanding where we are and where we want to go.

Our verse describes the sea as "ceasing from its raging." The Hebrew word *mizapo* (from its raging) occurs in the Bible thirteen times, but this is the only time it is used to describe the sea. Everywhere else it is used to describe a person or God. Ibn Ezra provides one example. "*And it,* [this word, is similar in meaning] *to 'zoaphim, raging'*" (Genesis 40:6). There it is used to describe the troubled state of Pharaoh's butler and baker the morning after their visionary dreams.

When we want our lives to cease from their raging, we can follow the examples of the sailors on the ship by trying out solutions, slowly and carefully. The midrash above from Pirke de Rebbi Eliezer says that they dipped Jonah into the water three times. We can take small steps and test the waters before we fully commit to taking life-transforming steps.

20

Human Kindness

How Can We Serve God through Simple Acts?

And the men feared the Eternal greatly; they offered a sacrifice
to the Eternal. And they made vows. —JONAH 1:16

The text tells us that the sailors offered sacrifices to the Eternal, but
it does not tell us when or how. We might conclude that they offered
the sacrifices immediately after the storm stopped, but what did
they have on board to sacrifice? Ibn Ezra explains that they offered
a sacrifice "after they left the ship," when they were able to obtain
an animal to sacrifice.

The text does not explicitly tell us the content of the sailors' vows.
Rashi explains that, combined with the awe and the offerings of the
earlier portions of the verse, these vows should be understood as
expressing the sailors' commitment to serving the God of the Israelites. They swore "that they would convert" to become worshippers
of the One God of Israel.

Kimchi sees the phrases "And they offered a sacrifice to the Eternal. And they made vows" as referring to two distinct acts. This vow
refers to "other oaths beyond their pledge to offer an offering such
as giving *tzedaka* to poor people."

Abarbanel sees these vows in the context of the general practice
of seafarers: "after they saw the strength of His providence and the
greatness of His miracles. And they vowed vows to offer sacrifices
according to the custom of those who go down to the sea in ships
when they go down into them." The general practice is for sailors to
promise to offer sacrifices upon their safe return. Here these sailors
add to those general promises new vows—to offer additional sacrifices upon their return.

Abarbanel turns to the midrash for an additional interpretation of this verse:

> And in Pirke de Rebbi Eliezer it says that they converted and returned to Jaffa and went up to Jerusalem and circumcised the flesh of their foreskins. The offering, which they offered at sea, is the covenant of circumcision that is like blood of the sacrifices. The sailors would first have to become Israelites before they could offer proper Israelite sacrifices. "And they made vows" to bring man, his wife, and the children and all that they have to the God of Jonah. And they made vows and fulfilled them. And concerning them it is written, "They who cling to empty folly forsake their own welfare" (Jonah 2:9).

Abarbanel takes this verse from Jonah's prayer from the belly of the fish in chapter 2 and uses it to describe the spiritual progress of the sailors here in chapter 1. He suggests that their original religion was folly.

The text repeats this phrase. The NJPS reflects the difference in context of the two verses. In verse 10 the NJPS renders it: "The men were greatly terrified." The NJPS translates the phrase here as "And the men feared greatly" and adds "the Eternal." The two uses of this phrase bracket the action, from when the sailors first learn of Jonah's misdeed to the resolution of the crisis. The text uses the same words twice, but they do not convey the same meaning. Earlier, in verse 10, they express the sailors' fear that the Eternal may cause their deaths as part of the punishment of Jonah. Here, in verse 16, they express the sailors' awe that the Eternal has saved them from death. And in verse 5, "the sailors cried out each to his own god," but here in verse 16 the sailors all present an offering to the Eternal, the One God of the Israelites. These verses describe the sailors' spiritual journey. As a result of their experience at sea, they have gained a new understanding of the Divine Presence in the world.

Most of our lives follow a less dramatic course than the sailors of our story. Nonetheless we also have opportunities to grow and experience the Divine. We do not have to be who we have always been. I have heard people make excuses for their behavior by saying, "That's just who I am." This is not an acceptable excuse for inaction, to be bitter, or to be constantly angry.

The events of our lives continue to shape us. Each experience impacts our sense of ourselves and the world around us. After a difficult event in our lives, we hear various aphorisms meant to comfort us. "What doesn't kill you makes you stronger" is a country song lyric, which might just be based on Friedrich Nietzsche's statement "Out of life's school of war: what does not destroy me makes me stronger" (*The Twilight of the Idols*).

We also hear, "God will never give you more than you can handle." This saying is likely based on Christian scripture, "God is faithful, and he will not let you be tested beyond your strength but with your testing he will also provide the way out so that you may be able to endure it" (1 Corinthians 10:13). I find neither of these common expressions of "wisdom" to be comforting.

Some of what does not kill us doesn't make us stronger; it weakens us physically and emotionally. We become wounded. We walk with a limp, literally or metaphorically. I have seen a mother visibly age from grief after her child died. I have watched protracted failure to find employment cause a friend to retreat from the world. And I do not believe that all that happens to be God's will. I see a great deal of randomness in the world. Natural occurrences, such as tornedos, earthquakes, and hurricanes, do not choose their victims. The evil acts of disturbed individuals setting bombs or shooting children in schools cannot be part of God's will. I refuse to see the ways in which disease strikes the young and the innocent as part of a Divine plan.

What does make us stronger? It isn't suffering. What makes us stronger is love: the love of our family, the love of our friends, the love of our community. I understand that some families are more loving and more lovable than others. Some of us make friends more easily than others. Some of us join groups more easily than others. To receive that love, we need to seed it. We cannot reap if we do not sow.

Years ago a synagogue in Chicago was defaced with swastikas. The next day's newspaper included a photo of the leaders of the congregation pointing at the swastikas. Later that week I saw one of the rabbis from the congregation. I remarked to him that if that had happened at our synagogue I would have rounded up my interfaith friends to stand with me. We would have had priests, ministers, and an imam pointing at the swastikas. He responded that they did not know the leaders of the other religious groups in their community. The rabbis of that congregation had made no effort to make friends with the interfaith community and therefore remained on the outside. As individuals, too, we need to be part of the community; we have to make an effort.

Public Action to Deliver Shelter is a project of eighty churches and our synagogue to provide food and shelter to the hungry and homeless of DuPage County. Each evening PADS has three shelter sites in the county. The social hall at my congregation, Etz Chaim, becomes a homeless shelter every Sunday evening. We feed our guests dinner, and they sleep overnight. We feed them breakfast and give them a bag lunch to take with them. Etz Chaim provides the volunteers for the first and fifth Sundays, and Christ the King Catholic Church does the second Sunday, and so forth. I am proud that a volunteer from Christ the King has a key to our building and the security code.

Our volunteers feel a strong sense of connection to each other, and the houses of worship feel a strong sense of community. When we decided to add on to our building, we needed to find a location for our High Holiday services that year. In our neighborhood, as often is the case, the Catholic Church has the largest sanctuary. Our member, Harve, spoke to Father Jim at Christ the King, asking him if we could rent their sanctuary. Father Jim said no. We could not rent their sanctuary, but we could use their sanctuary as their guests. Father Jim explained that we are partners in caring for the needy of our community and that we host the shelter every week. He added that this is what friends do for each other.

The sailors in our story changed as a result of their encounter with Jonah and God. They were transformed by witnessing the power of God to bring the storm and then to save them from it. In our lives we can see the power of our acts to transform us and the lives of those around us. I have seen countless members of our community embraced by others in the community in times of difficulty. We lift each other up. We make each other stronger. I see the presence of God in these simple acts of human kindness.

21

A Rickety Ladder

How Do We Understand the Suffering of the Innocent?

The Eternal provided a huge fish to swallow Jonah, and Jonah
remained in the fish's belly three days and three nights. —JONAH 2:1

At first reading, *provided* seems an odd word choice here. The verse
could have said that God directed the big fish or that God commanded
the big fish. In his commentary, Kimchi explains that the fish was
not present by random chance. It was part of God's plan. Kimchi
shows that the book of Daniel uses a form of this verb to describe
food that had been provided for Daniel.

> This is a matter of assignment. It is similar to "*manah*, allotted
> food and drink to you" (Daniel 1:10). The king assigned specific
> food to Daniel and the other selected youths of Judah. Ibn Ezra
> points out that "this is similar to summon." Kimchi explains "the
> God of Blessing assigned him, [the fish, to this task] for a specific
> time." At the [exact] time that Jonah was thrown into the sea, the
> fish was assigned [to be in the right spot] to swallow him. [And
> this fish is not] naturally in this sea.

In more of his commentary on this passage, Ibn Ezra explains that
those who want to discuss which species of fish are large enough
to accommodate a person for three days not only are incorrect but
they also miss the point of this story. He writes, "A person does
not have the strength to live in the belly of a fish for even an hour,
and for this number of days it is only possible by the means of a
miracle." Ibn Ezra views this entire incident as supernatural. God
intervened in the normal course of events on Earth to cause Jonah

to remain alive in the belly of the big fish that God had designated for this task.

Abarbanel seconds Ibn Ezra: "For a person could not exist in the belly of the fish, unless he is able to breathe cold wind, fresh air, from outside the fish. For there is nothing here to diminish faith in the miracle." And he compares it to the life of every human:

> And our eyes see that fetus resides in its mother's belly for nine months without eating, drinking, taking care of his needs, relieving himself, or breathing cold wind, fresh air, from outside. And what would prevent the Eternal from doing so for Jonah for those days? Does not the text [of the book of Daniel] give testimony that Chanania, Mishael, and Azariah [referred to by their Chaldean names Shadrach, Meshach, and Abed-Nego in the third chapter of Daniel] survived being "dropped bound, into the burning fiery furnace" (Daniel 3:23). And there is no doubt that following nature they would not have lived. For the burning hot air that would have consumed the moisture on which the roots of life depend and the wind would have killed them in an instant but the abilities of God transcend nature.

On Pesach we proudly proclaim that God took us out of Egypt "with a mighty hand and an outstretched arm" (Exodus 6:6). On Hanukah we sing, "Furiously they assailed us but Thine arm availed us. And Thy word broke their sword, when our own strength failed us" in "Maoz Tzur." In the Purim song "Utzu Eitza" we declare, "They have devised schemes, but they have been foiled, they have made declarations against us, but they will not be fulfilled, because God is with us!" But we know of times when our foes attacked us and God did not save us. We ask: Where was God during the Holocaust? Why did God not intervene in history to stop the destruction of the Jewish people? We are not the first generation to ask such questions. Medieval Jews asked why God did not intervene to prevent the Crusaders from slaughtering Jews in the Rhine valley? Ancient

Jews asked why God did not intervene to prevent the Romans from killing Jews in the first and second centuries.

In response, Kimchi draws upon a midrash to explain God's limited involvement in human history: "And this was one of the special category of miracles." And in Pirke de Rabbi Eliezer, Rabbi Tarfon says, "The fish was appointed from the sixth day of creation to swallow Jonah." The sages taught that wonders such as the big fish that occurred in the Bible were not contrary to nature but rather were built into the world as part of the act of creation. The sages suggest that these wonders, such as the dividing of the sea by Moses or the sun standing still in the sky for Joshua, were incorporated into creation by God on the afternoon of the sixth day (Genesis Rabbah 5:5 and Berachot 8a). Thus we should not see God as intervening in history on these occasions. Rather these wondrous events were part of the unfolding of nature as designed by God at the time of the creation of the world. Rather than focusing on God's role in the events of our lives on the grand scale of major historical events, we can seek to understand God's impact on our individual lives. Tractate Kiddushin in the Babylonian Talmud contains an interesting exploration of this topic. It first quotes the only two verses in the Torah that explicitly state the reward a person will receive from God for following a particular commandment.

> In the connection with the mitzvah of honoring one's father and mother it is written in the Torah, "Honor your father and your mother, as the Eternal your God has commanded you, that you long endure and that you may fare well" (Deuteronomy 5:16). And in connection with the mitzvah of sending a bird away from the nest before taking its young it is written in the Torah "that you may fare well and have a long life" (Deuteronomy 22:7).

Fulfilling these two commandments brings the same rewards: long life and that you may fare well. The Talmud tells a story of a boy who fulfilled both of these commandments. "There is the case of a boy whose father said to him, 'Climb up the tower and fetch me some young birds.' The son climbed up the tower, drove the mother away, and took the bird's offspring. On his way back down he fell and died." The Talmud asks, "Where is his good life? Where is his long life?" The boy fulfills the two commandments that should lead to long life: he honors his father by obeying his father's instructions, and he drives the mother bird away from the nest. Then he immediately dies. How can that be? Why doesn't God reward him for following the two commandments? The rabbis offer three explanations. The first rabbi suggests that the boy will be rewarded in the afterlife. The second rabbi suggests that perhaps at the moment he fell the boy was thinking about committing a sin. The third rabbi avoids theological gymnastics; he simply says, "Perhaps it was a rickety ladder. And whenever the potential for harm is present, we do not rely on miracles to save us."

This last response does not explain why God caused the boy to die: rather, it argues that God did not cause the boy's death. The boy died because he climbed a rickety ladder. Our situation in the world is like the little boy climbing a rickety ladder. As God did not cause the boy to fall, and God did not cause other victims to die. As God could not intervene in history to save the boy, God could not intervene in history to save the other victims. As the Talmud passage asserts, "And whenever the potential for harm is present, we do not rely on miracles to save us."

When we climb a rickety ladder, we may fall. When we walk near a rickety ladder, someone may fall on us. In some situations we can identify the rickety ladder and avoid climbing it or walking near it. In other situations we do not perceive the rickety status of our situation.

In this world we suffer and benefit from the choices we and other people make. I do not believe that God manages the events of our individual lives or the events of the world. While God provided a big fish to save Jonah, we cannot expect that God will provide a big fish or its equivalent to save us.

If that is true, what role does God play in our lives? I do not believe that God pulls all the strings, but that does not mean that God is irrelevant. I feel God to be present in my life every day. God is a source of strength, a source of courage, a source of right and wrong. God does change our lives. God is the Higher power that gives us the means to change our lives. God cannot change us, but God can help us change ourselves.

22

Telling Our Story

What Swallowed Jonah, a Fish or a Whale?

> The Eternal provided a huge fish to swallow Jonah, and Jonah
> remained in the fish's belly three days and three nights. —JONAH 2:1

During the song "Tradition," which opens *Fiddler on the Roof,* Tevye
says, "And among ourselves, we get along perfectly well. Of course,
there was the time when he sold him a horse, but delivered a mule,
but that's all settled now. Now we live in simple peace and harmony."
A man yells out, "It was a horse." Another man responds, "It was a
mule." The chorus echoes the dispute, "Horse! Mule! Horse! Mule!"
before joining in the refrain, "Tradition, tradition . . . tradition."

Our verse here uses the term *dag,* the masculine form for fish,
to describe the creature. And then the next verse, 2:2, reads that
Jonah is in the belly of a *dagah,* feminine form. Rashi, drawing on a
midrash, seeks to reconcile this apparent grammatical contradiction:

> It was a male [fish] and he could stand in an open space [in the
> belly of the fish], and so he was not moved to pray. The Holy
> One of Blessing intimated to the male fish and it spit him into
> the mouth of a female [fish], which was full of embryos [which
> pressed against the belly of the fish, decreasing the room available
> to Jonah]. There he was stressed and he prayed there, as it says
> in verse 2, "from the belly of the [female] fish *(mimai hadagah)."*

Ibn Ezra finds this fanciful midrashic rationalization unnecessary. "There is a person who says that the feminine fish swallowed
him from the mouth of the masculine fish. There is no need for
this complex explanation. For *dag* and *dagah* are nouns without

distinction as to gender, like *tzedek* and *tzedakah*. They can be used interchangeably."

Kimchi supporting Ibn Ezra's position looks for other biblical uses of the word *dag/ah*. This word appears in the Bible in the masculine and in the feminine; for example, "And the fish, *dagah*, that are in the Nile will die" (Exodus 7:18). The feminine *dagah*, here in this verse, is from the description of what will take place during the first plague, clearly refers to all fish. The text should certainly not be understood to say that when the Nile is turned into blood the female fish will die but the male fish will survive. While we may find Rashi's fanciful explanation entertaining, I think Ibn Ezra and Kimchi are more intellectually satisfying.

The original Hebrew describes the water dwelling creature that swallows Jonah as *dag gadol,* "big fish" or "great fish." Nonetheless, many people think of Jonah as having been in the belly of a whale, and there are many references to Jonah "in the belly of the whale." Father Mapple, the preacher in the whalers' church in *Moby Dick*, delivers a sermon in which he refers to Jonah in "the belly of the whale." This image of "the whale" comes from the translation of the Hebrew text into Greek and Latin and then into English. The Gospel according to Matthew 12:40 mentions Jonah's three days and three nights in the belly of the whale, foretelling the three days and three nights that the body of Jesus will be in the cave.

The Greek translation of the Hebrew Bible, the Septuagint, renders *dag gadol* as *ketos kegas, a big water dwelling creature.* In Jerome's translation of Jonah 2:1 into Latin, he describes Jonah as being in a *piscis granda*, a big fish. The original Greek version of Matthew uses *Ketos* to describe the creature that swallowed Jonah. Jerome translates it into Latin as *cetus.* Jerome translated Jonah from Hebrew into Latin, and he translated Matthew from Greek into Latin. And he uses two different words to describe the creature that swallowed Jonah. Jerome's inconsistency in Latin leads to the inconsistency in the King James Version.

The early English translations maintain this distinction, for in the KJV Jonah 2:1 reads, "Now the Lord had prepared a great fish to swallow up Jonah," and Matthew 12:40 renders it, "For as Jonas was three days and three nights in the whale's belly, so shall the Son of man be three days and three nights in the heart of the earth." Medieval art portrays Jonah both ways. In some paintings he is depicted as in the belly of a whale and in other times in a fish. On the ceiling of the Sistine Chapel, Michelangelo has placed Jonah at the head of the chapel over the altar with a big fish with gills at his sides. Children's books and cartoons usually have Jonah swallowed by a whale.

What is at stake in this Fish vs. Whale debate? I recognize that many people would respond, "Not much." I do not see any large theological points turning on whether it is a fish or a whale. But I do see a question of who owns the narrative. Whose story is it? Is it Matthew's story with a footnote to Jonah? Or is it Jonah's story with a footnote to Matthew? Is it a Jewish story that Christians also use for their own purposes? Or is it a Christian story with a Jewish foundation?

Each family has famous stories that are told and retold. We hear slightly different versions of the same story depending on who is telling the story. There are many ways to bend stories. Some people exaggerate, and some bend the stories so that they're in the middle of the action. How we tell the story becomes *the* story.

Communities also have stories. Take my congregation and its stories of its early years, for example. I was not there for those formative years, but I have heard the stories so many times that I feel I was part of them. I can even tell the stories about all the rented spaces we used before we moved into our own building. I am not certain that my versions are historically accurate, but I am confident that they portray the congregation in the way we want to be seen.

An early step in community organizing is to sit with another person and say, "Tell me your story." We have a story of our lives that makes sense out of the many episodes of our lives and in shaping our own narrative. We ignore certain events and embellish others. When we change the story that we tell others in order to improve it, we create a tension with the story we tell ourselves. Our real goal is to bring those two versions of our narrative into alignment. When we use "big fish" with others and "whale" with ourselves, problems arise with our sense of self. When someone asks us, "Tell me your story," let us respond with a narrative that describes our core values and the actual direction of our lives.

~~~~~~

23

Nothing Left to Lose

When Do We Turn to God?

Jonah prayed to the Eternal his God from the
belly of the fish. —JONAH 2:2

This verse introduces the central section of chapter 2, verses 3–10,
which contains Jonah's prayer. In verse 11, God commands the fish
to return Jonah to dry land. In their reflections on this verse, the
commentators speak about the prayer as a whole and provide us with
an opportunity to better understand the meaning of prayer and to
explore our experience of praying.

Ibn Ezra believes that the order in which the events are described
in the chapter reflects the sequence in which they actually occurred:
Jonah prayed and then he was released. But other commentators
argue that Jonah did not recite the prayer until he was already back
on dry land. Ibn Ezra explains:

The commentators wish to explain [the text by means of a] new
idea and remove the text from its plain meaning by saying that
Jonah did not pray until after he had gone out of the fish and onto
dry land. They base this interpretation on the preposition *mem,*
which they found preceding the word for "belly," since the text
reads "*mim'ei,* from the belly," not "*b'ma'ei,* in the belly." [They
argue that Jonah must have already been saved "from the belly"
when he prayed.] Did they not see that there in the text [in verse
3, it is written], "From the belly . . . I cried out." This is similar to
"Out of the depths I cried out to You, O Eternal" (Psalms 130:1).
Additionally the word for "I cried out" is a sign that he prayed and
cried out before the fish vomited him. And similarly in verse 8

of this chapter Jonah uses the future tense to describe his prayer reaching God: "My prayer will come before you." And if these commentators are correct, why is it not written here in verse 2, "And Jonah prayed after he went out of the belly of the fish"? In addition after his prayer it is written, "And the Eternal commanded the fish and it spewed Jonah out upon dry land." (Jonah 2:11)

Ibn Ezra argues that the text clearly places these two events, the prayer and the return to land, in proper sequence. "For God brought him into this difficult situation in order to save him from sin." [God provides Jonah with the opportunity to repent and seek forgiveness. And in response to his situation Jonah declares], "My prayer will come before you" (Jonah 2:8).

Another basis for arguing that Jonah recited the prayer after his deliverance is that the verbs in the prayer are in the past tense. For example in verse 3 Jonah says, "I called, *karati*." Ibn Ezra provides nine examples in which the Bible uses past tense verbs to describe events that have not yet taken place. He argues that these words are said in "the spirit of prophecy." So these events are understood as events that without a doubt will take place; therefore, they are spoken of in the past tense as if they had already occurred. We can look at two examples of Ibn Ezra's proof texts. "Which I wrested from the hand of the Amorites with my sword and my bow" (Genesis 48:22). In the blessing of Joseph's sons, Jacob speaks of what their descendants will one day inherit. This "taking of the land of the Amorites" does not occur until the time of Joshua; nevertheless, Jacob uses the past tense to describe it. "For an event which has been decreed by God to happen can be spoken of in the past tense."

"But Jeshurun grew fat and kicked" (Deuteronomy 32:15) and "God saw and was vexed and spurned His son" (Deuteronomy 32:19). These are words from the Song of Moses, through which Moses tells the story of the people of Israel including the future events which will befall them. In both verses we see past tense verbs describing events that have not yet taken place.

Rashi says that the words *holy palace* refer to the Temple in Jeru-salem. And that Jonah is speaking of again being able to see the Temple in Jerusalem. "I see now that you have kept me alive all these days; therefore, I know that I will again gaze at your Holy Temple."

Ibn Ezra disagrees; he contends that Jonah in the belly of the fish is not thinking about seeing the Temple in Jerusalem but rather sur-viving his ordeal and again seeing the sky. He draws upon a verse from Psalms to show that in the Bible, God's "holy palace" is under-stood to be in the heavens. "For the Eternal is in His holy palace." (Psalms 11:4). The second half of the verse locates God's throne in the heavens. If we assume that the throne is in the palace, we can conclude that God's palace is in the heavens. Ibn Ezra provides his source for this opinion. "And Rabbi [Yehudah Halevi explains it] in this manner." If *holy palace* refers to the Temple in Jerusalem, then these words could have been spoken by Jonah only after his return to dry land. If the phrase refers to the sky, it could only have been said from the belly of the fish. And there, in verse 10, it is written, "Salvation from the Eternal." In this concluding phrase of Jonah's prayer, he speaks of offering sacrifices in fulfillment of his vows and in response to God's act of salvation. The problem, which Ibn Ezra addresses, is that if the prayer was recited while Jonah was still in the fish's belly, the salvation had not yet taken place when Jonah spoke. According to Ibn Ezra's understanding, salvation from the Eternal is not what has already taken place. "This was his hope. 'Salvation from the Eternal' is what he was seeking."

When Jonah first arrives in the belly of the fish, does he believe that he is saved? Or does he believe that he is dying? The text offers no answer; the Bible rarely tells us what its characters think or feel; it is left up to us to imagine. I think that at first Jonah is not sure how to understand his situation, but on the third day, when he is still alive and unharmed, he realizes that salvation is his.

The text does not tell us when during the three days Jonah begins to pray. The prayer contained in verses 3–10 is a single unit and ideas flow without interruption from verse to verse, describing Jonah's descent, his repentance, and his devotion to God who saves him. As I read it, Jonah offered his prayer on the third day, followed immediately by God's instruction to the fish to return him to dry land. The prayers that Jonah offers to God are the words of a confident servant of the Eternal. During these three days in the belly of the fish, Jonah changes from a fugitive in flight into a prophet prepared to resume his mission.

Jonah has nothing left to lose. Jonah has no escape, so he turns to God.

The text tells us that Jonah directs his prayer "To the Eternal his God." Why does the text include both "the Eternal" and "his God"? This is the first time the book of Jonah uses the expression "his God." The Eternal is the name of the deity Jonah addresses. The use of "his God" declares that he sees himself in relationship with that deity now. He recognizes that being alive in the belly of the fish is not an accident but a step toward his salvation. Despite Jonah's flight, God remains focused on him. Jonah now turns to God.

When do we turn to our God? When we are confident or when we are troubled? As we read Jonah's prayer, let's imagine our prayers to God. What do we want from God? God is not the "Genie of the Lamp." God does not offer us "Three Magic Wishes." When we recite the prayers of the Siddur, we remind ourselves that our God can be our source of strength. We remember that God grants us knowledge and teaches us wisdom. We proclaim that our purpose is to perfect the world under God's protection.

24

Happy Thanksgiving

Why Should We Care about Other People?

He said: "In my trouble, *mtzarah*, I called to the Eternal,
and He answered me; From the belly of Sheol I cried
out, And You heard my voice." —JONAH 2:3

Many of the words in Jonah's prayer are from the book of Psalms and
so are rooted in well-known prayer language. The author of the book
of Jonah bases verse 3 on Psalms 120:1: "In my distress, *btzarah*, I
called to the Lord and He answered me." In Hebrew *mtzarah* in the
Jonah verse and *btzarah* in the Psalms verse are virtually the same
word. We should not be distracted by the difference in the English
between "trouble" and "distress." The author of Jonah accurately
quotes from Psalms to give Jonah's prayer additional gravitas.

Note that the second half of the verse is parallel in meaning to the
first half of the verse; it repeats the ideas conveyed. Scholars call this
Synonymous Parallelism. This is a very common form of biblical
poetry found throughout the wisdom literature and in poetic sections
of biblical narratives such as Moses' Song of Farewell in Deuteronomy 32:1–43 and the Song of the Sea in Exodus 15:1–18. For example,
Exodus 15:4 reads: "Pharaoh's chariots and his host He cast into the
sea, and his chosen officers were sunk in the Red Sea." It is easy to
see in this verse that the "B" part of the verse expresses the same
thoughts as the "A" part of the verse but in slightly different words.

In our verse from Jonah we can see that "From the belly of Sheol
I cried out" is parallel to "I called from my distress" and that "You
heard my voice" is parallel to "He answered me." The shift from
"in my distress *(btzarah lee)*" to "from my distress *(meetzarah lee)*"

strengthens the parallelism with "From the belly of Sheol," and doesn't significantly affect the meaning of the phrase.

Throughout the prayer Jonah speaks in the past tense, as if his rescue from the sea is complete and he has returned to dry land. It would make more sense to have this be in the present and future tenses: "I call upon the Eternal, and He will answer me." Perhaps Jonah speaks in the past tense because he saw himself saved from the moment the fish swallowed him and that he speaks of God's salvific acts as already completed because of his total confidence in God. Kimchi supports this interpretation: "Even though he stood in His creature he knew that he would exit the belly of the fish in peace." Or perhaps the tense of the verbs of the prayer grows out of the fact that the verses quoted from the book of Psalms were written in the past tense. The author of Jonah simply maintains the form of the verbs and matches his/her new composition to the Psalms' verbs.

Jonah says that he called to God from Sheol, yet he is not in Sheol but rather in the belly of the fish. Ibn Ezra explains that "Sheol is a deep dark place which is the opposite of the heavens which are on high." Jonah is as distant from God as a person can be.

In the belly of the fish Jonah is literally and spiritually in the depths. The Bible often uses the term *Sheol* to describe the destination of those who have died, as in Hannah's prayer in I Samuel 2:6, "The Eternal deals death and gives life / Casts down into Sheol and raises up." In Psalms 18:6 "the ropes of Sheol" are presented as parallel to "the snares of Death." The Hebrew Bible uses the term *Sheol* to describe the depths of the earth, a place far from God.

Many ancient religions share such an image of a lower world to which the dead go. In Greek mythology the underworld lies across the river Styx, often called Hades after the god who ruled there. But Hades is not the same as Sheol. In mythology Hades is a place; recall the myth in which Orpheus enters Hades to attempt to rescue Eurydice from the underworld. Sheol is understood as a biblical metaphor for the destination of the dead, not a physical location. Here in our verse, Jonah declares that he was near death, but now he has been rescued from the sea and so he thanks God. The verse does not speak of general distress. Jonah calls out to God as a result of his very specific pain. Jonah owns the trouble. The world is filled with troubles. We each have our specific troubles. Some troubles appear suddenly, like disease. But many of us have troubles that seem to follow us wherever we go, as Mississippi John Hurt sang: "Trouble, trouble, trouble had it all my days. Trouble, trouble, trouble had it all my days. Seem like trouble gonna carry me to my grave." Some people feel that their lives take them from one disappointment to another. As the old country song proclaims, "I am a man of constant sorrow. I've seen trouble all my day."

Jonah calls out to God. Some people keep their pain to themselves. They do not cry out to God or to other people; they shut down in their distress, isolate themselves, and spiral downward. What prevents a person from crying out? In their isolation and fear, they imagine that no one will respond to their cry. Yet if only people knew of their suffering, they might get help. There can be no response until the person cries out. Other people don't admit to their distress because they think it would be seen as a sign of weakness. They fear that other people would look down at them.

Once Jonah calls out to God from the belly of the big fish, he is no longer alone.

When we call out from our depths, we are no longer alone. And when we respond to the call of another, they are no longer alone.

A member of my congregation, David, told me the following story: He once worked as a social worker at a residential facility for people with serious problems. One patient suffering from serious depression refused to speak to anyone at any time. On Thanksgiving morning David took some time to walk around the facility wishing all the patients a Happy Thanksgiving before joining his family for their celebration. He stopped in front of this depressed man and wished him a Happy Thanksgiving. To David's surprise the man responded, "Happy Thanksgiving." He explained that he understood that David had come to visit on his own time on that holiday morning. By visiting on Thanksgiving, David demonstrated to this previously silent man that he cared about him.

Folksinger John Prine describes isolated people: "Waiting for someone to say, 'Hello in there, hello.'" We need to be ready to respond to the call of others, as God was ready to respond to the call of Jonah. And when they do not have the power to speak, we need to begin the conversation.

25

Strong Waves and Big Rocks

What Overwhelms Us?

"You cast me into the depths, / Into the very heart of
the seas, / The floods engulfed me; / All your breakers
and billows/ Swept over me." —JONAH 2:4

The author of the book of Jonah took the second half of this verse,
"all your breakers and billows swept over me," from Psalms 42:8
(42:7 in some English translations). The Psalmist is not describing
a person actually in the sea. The Psalmist uses the phrase as part of
a poetic image to describe the feelings of a person far from Jerusalem. Our author recognizes that Jonah could say these words, and
so he constructs the first half of the Jonah verse to be in parallel with
this phrase from Psalms.

Our author assumes that readers of the book of Jonah will recognize
the quote from Psalms. The ancient Israelites knew the Psalms like
we know popular song lyrics today. People of my generation would
be able to complete the phrase, "The answer my friends is . . ." (Bob
Dylan). Those familiar with classic Broadway musicals would have
no problem with "I got the horse right here . . ." (Frank Loesser, *Guys
and Dolls*). And fans of the Grateful Dead would immediately be able
to complete "Some time the light's all shining on me . . ." (Robert
Hunter). Our commentators' remarks on this passage center on particular words. Ibn Ezra explains why the text uses the plural form of
the word *seas*, even though it is clear that Jonah is only in one sea: "It
is like 'on your Niles'" (Exodus 7:19). As there is only one Nile there
in the book of Exodus, so there is only one sea here in the book of
Jonah. In Hebrew the plural form can be used poetically to refer to

the singular. Ibn Ezra then turns to another possibility: "Yafet [ben Ali] says that the Sea of Reeds mixes with the Sea of Yaffo."

While the English word *breakers* is commonly used for *waves*, its use for this purpose in biblical Hebrew is unprecedented, so the commentators feel obliged to explain it. Rashi writes: "All the waves of the sea are called breakers because they break and divide the sea." Kimchi adds: "In the breaking of the waves of the sea at the moment they billow, they are called breakers." And Abarbanel explains "swept over me" this way: "For he descended under the sea, and the waves and the breakers on the surface of the sea passed over him."

The text addressed to God says, "You cast me into the sea." We know that the sailors actually cast Jonah into the sea, but they did so as God's agents. In our lives we at times feel cast into the depths by the weather, by world events, and by other people. People close to us have the greatest power to cast us into the depths, and often so do people in positions of power.

As a young rabbi, when was I most anxious leading services? When my parents came to visit or when there was another rabbi in the congregation. I wanted my parents to view me, their little boy, as a competent professional, someone of accomplishment. I wanted my peers to see me as worthy of their collegial respect and admiration. I wanted my parents *and* my colleagues to view me as a legitimate rabbi. Their opinions affected how I saw myself; disapproval from my parents or my colleagues could have "cast me into the depths" of self-doubt.

Sometimes people who hold positions of power evaluate us unfairly. In high school I joined the debate team, and we competed with other high school teams in tournaments. In the classroom to which our team was assigned there would be me and my teammate Larry, our two opponents, and a teacher/coach from a third neutral school serving as the judge. One morning as I stood up to speak, I looked at the judge. Believe it or not, he had fallen asleep. I subtly tried to wake him by speaking louder, but he remained asleep. I looked at Larry. I looked at the members of the other team. All responded with amused grins; nobody wanted to get up and wake him. So I just continued on. At the end of the day we received a poor evaluation and low points from the sleeping judge. He did not hear me speak, yet he gave me a disappointing grade. I felt "cast into the depths."

Many rabbis complain about the pressure they feel from the lay leaders of the congregation. I once heard a rabbi describe his president as "Sluggo," and it seems that he had honestly earned this nickname. That's not the kind of synagogue president I want to work with, so when I meet with a new president I imagine that I am sitting down with my new best friend. I tell new presidents that I will never surprise them, and I ask them never to surprise me. I also suggest that it would be best for the congregation if we could work out any disagreements we have in private rather in public. In over thirty years at my congregation I have never had a fight or even a heated disagreement with a president. We do not always agree, but we always can work things out. I will not let a congregational president cast me into the depths. I will never let our communications become like a wave hitting rocks. We work together on the same team.

We do not have close votes at our board meetings because we like to build consensus on important issues. Over the years, I have had ideas that I believed were well thought out and good for the congregation, but others did not always share my "enlightened" point of view. How we say the Mourners Kaddish is a case in point. Our congregation, like many Reform congregations, has the custom of the entire congregation standing during Kaddish. After my father, *alav hashalom,* died I recited Kaddish during the first year and on his *yahrzeit.* But as I did so I felt that everyone standing with me, reciting all together, diminished the significance for me as a mourner. I proposed to the congregation that we change our practice and adopt the more traditional custom of having just the mourners stand.

I presented this proposal to the full congregation during a High Holiday sermon and then took it up with the Ritual Committee. To my surprise the congregation was quite divided on the question. Some argued that we all stood to recite Kaddish for Holocaust victims who did not have surviving relatives. Others argued that many people would be uncomfortable standing to recite the Kaddish while most others sat because they were not confident of their ability to recite the words correctly. It became clear to me that I could only carry the day through force of personality, and I didn't want to resolve the matter that way, so I dropped the proposal. I didn't want to let the congregation cast me into the depths. And I do not want to cast the leaders of the congregation into the depths. I will never let our communications become like a wave hitting rocks; we work together on the same team.

On the personal level, I do not want to be driven onto the rocks by strong waves. Also I do not want to be the strong wave driving someone else onto the rocks. I am a big fellow with a loud voice in a position of leadership. I need to be careful that I do not let myself become a strong wave driving someone else into the big rocks.

26

I Once Was Lost, but Now I'm Found

How Can We Grow?

"I thought, 'I was driven away / Out of your sight: / Would I ever gaze again / Upon Your holy Temple?'" —JONAH 2:5

Here again, as in the last chapter's verse, the author draws upon Psalms 31:23 (31:22 in some English translations). The Hebrew Psalms passage reads, *V'Ani amarti v'chaftzi nigrazti mineged einech* (And I said in my alarm, 'I was cut off from before your eyes'). Jonah's author drops *v'chaftzi* (in my alarm) and replaces *nigrazti* (I was cut off) with *nigrashti* (I was driven), since Jonah does want to express a total break with God. The author's use of the passive voice may seem curious. For in truth Jonah was not driven from God; he fled. The verse could have said, *brachti mineged einecha* (I fled from before your eyes), but the author may have chosen to use the passive form, *nigrashti* (I was driven) to maintain the sound and structure of the phrase in Psalms. The two Hebrew words have a very similar sound. Or perhaps the passive voice allows Jonah to avoid fully accepting responsibility for his situation.

Kimchi offers another explanation for the use of the passive verb. "I thought that when they threw me into the sea I was dead." Therefore I would have no further contact with You. I was driven from your presence by the act of the sailors. Clearly Jonah did not "say" these words as he was thrown into the sea: rather, he thought them. Rashi suggests that Jonah thought, "When they threw me into the sea I thought I was dead [or about to die] and therefore driven from your sight."

The Hebrew word *ach* connects the two halves of the verse. The straightforward way to translate *ach* is to render it *therefore*. However, the two halves seem to be in opposition to each other and more appropriately connected by *yet*, as here in Rashi's rendering: "I was driven from your sight yet I see now that you have kept me alive all these days."

Ibn Ezra explains how the verse expresses Jonah's spiritual shift:

> That is to say from when you kept watch over me, [when I served as a prophet], until I thought that You hid Your face and eyes from me [during my flight]. But now that You have performed this great miracle for me and I continue to be alive here in the belly of the fish I think that I will again be able to gaze upon your dwelling place of your holiness in the Temple and the place of prophecy and the place where you will watch over me. Cause me to return to it because I fled from it.

Abarbanel suggests that Jonah not only expresses confidence that he will reconnect to God through worship but also that he will again serve as a prophet: "The matter here is that when I, Jonah, descended to Yaffo to flee toward Tarshish, I knew I was removed from before you, I mean to say that [I believed that] prophecy would not again be initiated through me. But all my thoughts were vanity. For in truth I will again 'gaze upon Your holy Temple.' For God will compel prophecy to return to me."

Earlier, in chapter 5, I described Jonah's continuous descent, from Jerusalem down to Yaffo, then down to the port, then down to the hold of the ship and then down to the depths of the sea. In verse 7 we will read that the fish takes Jonah to the base of the mountains at the bottom of the sea. And there, Jonah renews his relationship with God.

The Christian hymn "Amazing Grace" (John Newton) expresses just such a dramatic shift in relationship with God. The words of this song describe a person far from God whose life is turned around by the divine gift of grace. "Amazing grace, how sweet the sound / That saved a wretch like me. / I once was lost, but now I'm found. / Was blind, but now I see."

People often look at the meaning of this hymn in the context of Newton's biography. Before entering the life of an Anglican worship leader and hymn composer, he served as a captain of a British ship in the slave trade, purchasing slaves in Africa to sell in the New World. On one voyage his ship became caught in a storm and Newton barely survived. This crisis moved him to reexamine his life; he gave up drinking, gambling, and cursing, and he gave up the slave trade. In folksinger Arlo Guthrie's telling of the tale on his album "Precious Friend," Newton turned his ship around and took the slaves back to Africa.

Newton's life change raises for us the possibility of turning our own lives around. We do not have to continue on our familiar path. If you always do what you have always done you will always get what you have always gotten. We can leave the familiar behind and boldly go where we have never gone before. Or perhaps we lost the sense of a path in our lives. In that case we can turn by returning to the path we have lost. No matter how far we feel that we have strayed from the path, there is a way to "get back to where we once belonged."

This hymn expresses the thrust of Jonah's prayer. In the belly of the fish at the bottom of the sea, Jonah imagines himself once again serving as a prophet of God. This turning, this *teshuva,* becomes the first step in Jonah's "salvation." Not the type of salvation described in "Amazing Grace," salvation in the world to come, but salvation in this world. For us to climb out of our own depths we first need a vision, a path. Before any conversation about the light at the end of the tunnel, we first have to be able to see that a tunnel exists that can lead us from where we are to where we want to be.

To turn his life around, Newton gave up drinking, gambling, cursing, and the slave trade. Jonah gave up fleeing from God. What do we need to do to turn our lives around? For most of us the change will be less dramatic than Newton's and Jonah's. It certainly might include giving up drinking or gambling. It might also be watching what we do or watching what we say. The food that goes into our mouths can be destructive to our health. The words that come out of our mouths can be destructive to others. If we look at ourselves honestly, we know the issues that challenge us and understand that we can do better.

27

Feeling Trapped

Is There a Way Out?

> "The waters closed in over me, the deep engulfed me;
> weeds twined around my head." —JONAH 2:6

The previous three verses contain contrasting phrases that describe Jonah's predicament in the belly of the big fish and his confidence in God's saving power. In contrast, all three phrases in the verse here speak only of Jonah's difficulty. This verse marks the thematic low point of Jonah's prayer. It does not express hope, only despair.

The last phrase of the verse captures the attention of the commentators. The image of the reeds tangled around Jonah's head raises a narrative problem. How could reeds be causing Jonah trouble while he is in the belly of the fish? The commentators offer a few responses.

Rashi, following the Targum, understands the term *reeds* in this text to refer to the "Sea of Reeds" rather than actual reeds. Therefore Jonah says, "The Sea of Reeds hangs from above my head." The Holy One of Blessing showed him the Sea of Reeds and how the Israelites crossed it. Rashi also explains how Jonah could see the Sea of Reeds from inside the belly of the fish. "The two eyes of the fish were like two windows and he looked out and saw all that was in the sea."

Kimchi contends that the text refers to actual reeds:

There is a type of reed that grows on the banks of the Nile and shores of the sea. Therefore the reeds that grow on the shores and banks are called great reeds. And there is a type that grows on the floor of the sea at the base of the mountains. And it is called *algae* in French. It is thin and long and it wraps around the heads of fish. And that is what happens here when it says, "The reeds wrapped around my head." The explanation of "My head" is "the head of the fish that swallowed me." For his head, Jonah's was like his, the fish's head all the time that he was in the fish.

Kimchi suggests that we should understand Jonah's mention of his own head to be a metaphor for the fish's head.

Abarbanel explains how the reeds become tangled on the head of the fish. "This is similar to the things which grow in the sea which plants acquire. And the reeds grow between them. And sometimes when the fish swim through the water these plants and reeds become tangled around their heads." The reeds, whether tangled about Jonah's head or the head of the fish, add to the image of Jonah being trapped.

The opening phrase of the verse is similar to *"ki ba'u mayim ad nefesh."* I would translate this literally as "For the water comes to [my] soul" from Psalms 69: 1(2). From the context of both verses, *my* can be inserted before *soul* to clarify the meaning. Ibn Ezra explains that this phrase should be understood to mean "Until my soul was about to die." Kimchi explains the poetic image and provides a similar use of this image from the book of Psalms. "The water swirled around me until my soul was about to depart and then the fish swallowed me." And similarly, in Psalms 69:1, "Until the waters have come unto my soul." Water was about to take Jonah's life.

As is often the case, the biblical text does not provide as many details as we would like. The text does not tell us how long Jonah was in the water before the fish swallowed him. Did Jonah hit the water at all? Perhaps the fish jumped out of the sea and swallowed Jonah in midair like a dolphin in a show at SeaWorld.

Kimchi paints a picture of Jonah about to drown before the fish saved him. He takes this portion of the verse to mean not the time that Jonah was in the belly of the fish but rather those moments before the fish swallowed him. Jonah was close to death when the fish swallowed him, and the fish saved him from drowning.

Jonah felt like there was no way out. He could not escape. He could no longer run away. He was completely trapped.

Many people face difficulties that create the feeling of being trapped. People feel trapped by relationships, by financial challenges, and by physical pain. Some people find themselves in marriages from which they believe they cannot extricate themselves. Some dig such a deep hole of debt that they cannot imagine a way to climb out.

I can share personal testimony about the impact of pain. For many years I experienced sciatica. The first time was during the Torah reading at a Shabbat morning service. Standing at the reading stand listening to the bar mitzvah boy chant his *maftir* portion, I felt a sharp pain running down my leg. I came to learn that this was not a leg problem but a back problem. Walking was possible, but standing still hurt. If I sat down, the pain went away instantly. Physical therapy solved the problem, but a few years later the pain returned. I had to conduct Rosh Hashanah services sitting on a barstool. Again a few weeks of physical therapy solved the problem. Two years later, the pain returned for a third time. This time it was different. Walking did not help. Sitting did not help. Lying on the floor helped a bit. Physical therapy did not solve the problem. I was not able to go upstairs to bed. I could not sit in a chair.

During this time my wife and I were scheduled to close on the refinancing of our mortgage. When the agent came to our house, I could not sit in a chair at a table to sign the documents, so he got down on the floor with me. He was not going to leave without closing. I am as positive and upbeat a person as lives, but during those days I was growing quite depressed. I felt that "the deep engulfed me." I felt that the pain encompassed my soul. While I did not literally have "reeds tangled about my head," I certainly was not thinking clearly. I could not imagine continuing to live in such pain.

When my wife drove me to the orthopedist, I lay down in the back of her suv. I wanted her to drive faster but also more smoothly. At the doctor's office I could not sit in a chair. I had to lie on the floor in the waiting room. The doctor told me that I had a herniated disc and would require surgery. Fortunately, he was able to schedule surgery for the next day. When I woke up in the recovery room, I knew right away that the pain was gone. I felt that I was reborn.

The second paragraph of the *amidah* describes God as "giving life to the dead." I gained a new understanding of these words through my back ordeal. Many people suffer with chronic problems and pain. As I have grown older, I have learned more and more about the fragility of the human body. I also appreciate that deep human need to seek a path to escape from that which entangles us. But I realize that some people cannot see a way out. The deep does engulf them every day of their lives. The deep may be a life-threatening illness. It might be chronic pain. It is in some cases isolation and fear. My back pain was alleviated by a surgical procedure doctors perform every day. For some conditions, no surgical response will work. We cannot count on a miracle like the one that saved Jonah.

So what do we do when our friends and relatives suffer in such a way? We are present for them. We let their tears fall on our shoulders. Tradition teaches us that when we make a *shiva* call, we should not ask the mourners, "How are you?" We know how they are. When we try to speak to mourners, we have difficulty finding the right words. The tradition says that we should not even speak until they speak. We comfort them not through the wisdom of our words but through the strength of our presence. The same holds true for visiting with friends who are suffering. We do not need to search for the right words that will bring them comfort and support. In truth the "right" words do not exist. We have already brought comfort and support just by showing up.

28

Recovering from a Perfect Storm

From Where Does Our Hope Come?

"I sank to the base (*l'kitzvei*) of the mountains. The bars of the
earth closed upon me (*va'adi*) forever. Yet You brought my
life up from the pit, O Eternal my God!" —JONAH 2:7

The Hebrew text uses the word *l'kitzvei* to describe a specific part
of the mountains. Its use here is difficult to understand. The word
generally means "cut." Ibn Ezra explains it as meaning "to the place
where the mountains are cut off. This is from the category of phrases
such as 'and he cut a tree at its base.'" Kimchi elaborates: "to the end
of the mountains that are in the sea. That is to say to their roots that
are at the floor of the sea in its extreme depth. And Targum Yonaton [the Aramaic translation of books of the Prophets] renders it, 'I
went down to the foundation of the mountains.' Rashi adds, 'to the
end [the bottom] of the height of mountains fixed in the depths of
the sea did I descend.'"

This first phrase of the verse describes the depths of Jonah's
descent. He is as low as one can go. At the beginning of chapter
1, Jonah stood in the mountains at the center of the country. He
descended to Jaffa. He went down to the harbor and down to a ship.
Once on board he climbed down into the hold of the ship. The sailors threw him into the sea. And now the big fish takes him "Twenty
Thousand Leagues under the Sea" (Jules Verne). Jonah has literally
reached the bottom of the earth.

I have met people who are metaphorically down as far as they
can go. We have a shelter for the homeless at our synagogue every
Sunday evening. Our guests come for dinner and in the morning
we feed them breakfast and provide a bag lunch for them to take

with them. Our homeless guests have no one else to whom they can turn. They do not have friends or relatives who can take them in. Some come from troubled families. They have no relatives in the position to offer shelter. Some have been abused or abandoned by people they trusted. Others have burned bridges connecting them to their relatives and their friends. In any case they have lost their jobs and lost their homes. Often they feel that there is no way out.

We get "low" in various ways through denial, procrastination, rationalization, anger, acting out, running away, alcohol, and drugs. Some people descend into mental illness. The way down tends to isolate us until eventually we end up like Jonah at sea in the middle of a "Perfect Storm" of despair. If we have not experienced this ourselves, we likely have seen it in others. Beat poet Allen Ginsberg described the descent of many of his contemporaries in his poem "Howl": "I saw the best minds of my generation destroyed by madness, starving hysterical naked, dragging themselves through the Negro streets at dawn looking for an angry fix."

What Jonah says in the second phrase of our verse does not seem to express a complete image. Again we have to unpack the Hebrew. Rashi suggests that it should be understood as the earth, its bars "against me from above are closed, I will not be able to ascend forever." The unclear word is *va'adi*. The root of the word *va'adi* is *bet-aiyin-daled*. Rashi draws our attention to a biblical example of the word *ba'ad* used with the word *sagar* to mean "closed after." *Va'adi* here in Jonah "is like *ba'adaich* in Second Kings 4:4 'Go in and shut the door *ba'adaich*, behind you and your children.' So it is with every instance of *ba'ad* in the Bible. 'Skin, *baad*, after skin' in Job 2:4 means a limb after a limb." Rashi argues that the use of *va'adi* in our text is consistent with its use in other places in the Bible. He says it always implies completed action after or against someone. In this context it means that it seems to Jonah that he will not be able to rise.

In the final phrase of this verse Jonah realizes he will be saved. Why does he describe his situation as being trapped for eternity? Rashi explains, "This is included in that which is written above [in

Jonah 2:5], 'I said I was driven away.' So we should understand this phrase as [earlier] I said, 'The land from which I fled is closed to me forever. [But now I know God will save me].'"

As he often does, Kimchi provides the equivalent of a voice-over narration. He imagines Jonah's thought process. "From the beginning I thought that the land, the dry land, its bars against me that is to say [the way to reach dry land] was barred against me. [I feared] that I would never be able to go up [to dry land]. And the sea would be my grave. And after I was alive in the belly of the fish I knew that I would escape from this pit alive and the pit would not be my grave but rather I would return to dry land."

Flying through the air, after the sailors threw him off the ship and before he hit the water, Jonah must have been thinking, this is the end of my life. I am going to drown in the sea. I am sure that when the fish began to swallow Jonah, he saw it as another punishment from God. Rather than just letting me quietly drown, God is bringing about my death through the more violent act of being eaten by a big fish. But he does not die. He finds himself alive in the belly of the fish. At some point he begins to understand that the fish is not part of his punishment but part of his salvation.

In chapter 1 of this book I shared Abarbanel's suggestion that Jonah was the unnamed boy that the prophet Elijah brought back to life, the widow's son (1 Kings 17:19–22). The midrash imagines that this anonymous boy is actually the young Jonah. In commenting on this verse, Abarbanel suggests that Jonah's positive attitude came from recalling "the miracle that was done for me in my childhood when Elijah brought me back to life."

How do we climb out of the depths in which we find ourselves? We cannot count on Divine intervention; God will not send a big fish to save us. But God can provide wisdom, strength, and courage. We need wisdom to honestly look at our situation. We need the strength to begin to climb out of the hole into which we have descended. We need the courage to avoid the traps that have ensnared us in the past. We need to decide that time for change has come.

When Rosa Parks refused to give up her seat to a white man on that bus in Montgomery, Alabama, in 1955, she sparked the Montgomery Bus Boycott. It became a milestone in the civil rights movement. Many historians view it as a pivotal moment in the birth of public demonstrations in support of civil rights.

What motivated Rosa Parks to act that day? In her autobiography she writes, "People always say that I didn't give up my seat because I was tired, but that isn't true. I was not tired physically, or no more tired than I usually was at the end of a working day. I was not old, although some people have an image of me as being old then. I was forty-two. No, the only tired I was, was tired of giving in." For us to strike out on a new path on our lives we too have to be "tired of giving in."

Every Saturday morning I hear a thirteen-year-old declare, "I am now an adult in the eyes of the Jewish community." It is an exaggeration; they are still children. But as real adults we do have to accept full responsibility for what we do. We have to accept responsibility for our lives. We have to acknowledge how we got so low. Then we can look for a path back up. We need to be able to visualize a better future, to hope.

Greek mythology explains the origins of hope. It is part of the story of the origin of evil. Pandora receives a lavishly decorated box as a wedding gift. She is also told that she absolutely must not open the box. But she cannot resist the temptation to look inside. She opens the box and all the evil hidden inside escapes and spreads throughout the earth. She struggles to close the box, but it is too late. Everything in the box has departed. Only one precious thing remains in the box, and that is hope.

We do not need to deny the seriousness of the challenges we face. We do not need to be able to prove that success seems likely. We do need to be able to create a vision in which we overcome all the obstacles and forces that appear to hold us back. We need hope.

Rabbi Arnold Jacob Wolf wrote, "Hope is not extrapolated from events, but always and inevitably imposed upon history. It comes despite, not because of, 'reality.' It is always a hope against hope" (*Sh'ma*, April 2, 1982). The confidence that our life situation can improve may not grow organically out of our life experience. In our individual lives we need to impose hope rather than wait for our experiences to create it. Hope illuminates the path from here to there. Hope is not the light at the end of tunnel. Hope lights up the interior of the tunnel, making it possible for us to move forward.

29

Seeking Community

How Can We Overcome Isolation?

"B'hitateif, in the wrapping upon me of my soul, I
called the Eternal to mind, and my prayer came before
You, into Your holy Temple." —JONAH 2:8

English translations of the book of Jonah render the opening phrase
of this verse as "When my life was ebbing away" (NJPS, ESV) or "When
my soul fainted within me" (KJV). These translations mask the difficulty that the original Hebrew poses. Translators, understandably,
feel an obligation to present a text that is clear even when the original
is not. Reading the explanations of the commentators we will see
how they move from the confusing or obscure original Hebrew to
providing the foundation for the clear English translations.

The first Hebrew word of the verse, *b'hitateif*, literally means "in
the wrapping." You may be familiar with this word from the blessing
said before wrapping yourself in your tallit. That blessing concludes
with the words *l'hitateif batzitzit*. Here in our verse, the image of
Jonah's soul wrapping upon him is difficult to understand.

Rashi draws upon the Targum's translation of this word into the
Aramaic *b'ishtal'hayut*, to provide the basis for his interpretation.
He explains that it is "in a swoon and thus the soul is wrapped
upon itself." Our word is in a *hitpa'ail* verb form, but Rashi provides an example of this root, in a *niphal* verb form, used to convey a similar meaning, in Lamentations 2:11, "The infant and baby
fainted, *bai'ateif*."

Ibn Ezra points out a biblical use of another form of the same
root, *eiyen-tet-fay*, to refer to fainting. "This is similar to 'as he is
faint, *ya'atof*'" (Psalms 102:1).

Kimchi takes a different approach. Rather than understanding "wrapping" as a metaphor for fainting, he reads this phrase as a description of the impact of suffering on the length of one's life. "This is the language that speaks about most of the suffering that shortens the soul [the life] of a person and thus their soul is wrapped up in it." Kimchi imagines Jonah thinking, "When the fish swallowed me, immediately I thought I would die."

Ibn Ezra connects *"my soul"* from this verse with "my life" from the previous verse. "This is in the manner of metaphor concerning his soul that in truth is his life." When Jonah says his soul is wrapping in on itself he means that he felt himself to be close to death. Believing that the end of his life was quickly drawing near, Jonah appeals to God.

How do other people respond when they think that their death is near? Some utter "famous last words." We recall some of these words because they summarize the speaker's life or because they contain a clever turn of phrase. We all know Revolutionary War patriot Nathan Hale's heroic last words: "I only regret that I have but one life to lose for my country." Roman emperor Augustus boasted about the transformation of Rome during his reign: "I found Rome brick, I leave it marble." Former president John Adams expressed regret concerning his lifelong rival: "Thomas Jefferson still survives." (As it happens, Jefferson had died a few hours earlier on the same day, July 4, 1826, exactly fifty years after the signing of the Declaration of Independence.) Battling what turned out to be a fatal illness, Lady Nancy Astor regained consciousness. Seeing her relatives gathered around her, she wittily asked, "Am I dying, or is this my birthday?"

Jonah does not offer clever "last words," as he believes his death to be imminent. He says that as his life was ebbing away he turned his thoughts to God. Kimchi suggests that Jonah thought, "Even so I remembered the God of Blessing and prayed to him."

Early in that wonderful film *Monty Python and the Holy Grail*, we see a man pushing a cart through a village deeply ravaged by the plague. The man cries out, "Bring out your dead. Bring out your dead." A man delivers a body to the mortician. But the supposedly dead man yells out, "I'm not dead yet." In the second half of our verse Jonah, in his own way, cries out, "I'm not dead yet."

As Jonah turns his attention to God, his outlook shifts from despair to confidence as we see in the second half of the verse. Kimchi imagines Jonah thinking, "Since I remained alive in the belly of the fish I knew that my prayer would come to you." Jonah concludes that God is paying attention to him from the miraculous manner in which a fish saved him from drowning. Therefore he can be confident that his prayer will indeed come before God. As this verse concludes, he no longer feels lost or close to death.

How does our outlook change when we pray? What are we doing when we pray? Some people turn to God in prayer with specific requests. They ask God to intervene in their lives to save them or a loved one. They ask God to provide what is missing.

Jewish prayer tends to be less focused on our individual needs. When we pray we proclaim that we are not alone. The words of our prayers describe God's relationship with the world and our relationship with God. We describe God "as the one Who every day continually renews the work of creation." We express our commitment to love God "with all our hearts, with all our souls, and with all our might."

As Jews we do not pray alone. We pray with a *minyan,* ten people to form a group for prayer. We connect with the Divine and with other people at the same time. As we speak to God, we hear the voices of the other members of the *minyan* also speaking to God. We become part of a praying community. A basic human need is to be part of a community. Isolation drains our souls. Cynics may say talking to yourself is a conversation with someone who cares. I observe that people who remain detached from others become bitter rather than sweet.

Why do people self-isolate? We may fear other people. We may fear that they are judging us. We can devote significant time and energy to stewing about what they think of us. We care too much about what people will say, and we allow these imagined judgments to prevent us from connecting to others. We may not have confidence in ourselves.

Too many times I have seen people withdraw because they no longer could present themselves to the public as they once did. Health setbacks cause people to lose the ability to speak as clearly as they once did or to walk confidently without help. They stay home alone so that no one will see them in their weakened condition. In Pirke Avot 2:5 we read Hillel's words, "Do not distance yourself from the community." Hillel teaches us not to step away from others. We should be stepping toward others.

As a community we should not allow these once active treasured members to isolate themselves. Every new chair of our congregation's Caring Committee hears me explain how we should model our caring efforts after the example of the Cook County Democratic Party of the Mayor Richard Daley era. We should have a structure of ward captains, precinct captains, and block captains. I do not advocate using the same terminology, but just as the old party block captains would stay in touch with all the residents in their blocks, the congregation's neighborhood captains should stay in touch with our members in their neighborhood. When members face difficulty, we should not have to wait for them to call us. Our caring structure should already know.

New members of the congregation should not be allowed to stay at the fringe of the community. We need to personally invite them to come to activities and to introduce them to other members in their neighborhood or in similar life situations.

Every Friday evening at our services we have official greeters standing right inside the entrance to our building. They welcome newcomers and say hello to longtime members. On Friday evenings everyone wears a name tag. This allows all of us to greet each other by name, people we have just met, people we sort of know, as well as our longtime friends. Everyone who walks through our doors should feel appreciated, understood, and treasured by the community. They should feel part of our sacred community just as Jonah feels reconnected to God through his prayer.

30

Don't Look Back

How Can We Avoid the Traps of the Past?

They who cling to empty folly forsake their own welfare. —JONAH 2:9

The opening phrase of the verse "*m'shamrim havlei shav,* They who cling to empty folly" is similar to "*hashomrim havlei shav,* those who rely on empty folly" in Psalms 31:7(6). The author changes *hashomrim,* in the *kal* conjugation, into *m'shamrim,* in the *pi'el* conjugation. Verbs in the *pi'el* conjugation usually indicate intensive action. Translating *m'shamrim* as "they who cling" or "those who zealously serve" expresses the distinction between the *kal* and *pi'el* forms. While the Hebrew Bible often uses this root, *shin-mem-reish,* it appears in the *pi'el* form only once in the Hebrew Bible: here in our verse. Our author created this unique usage to describe the intensity of the devotion here to the "empty folly." The text does not explicitly tell us to whom this refers. The commentators attempt to resolve this mystery.

Rashi tells us that this phrase refers to the sailors as "they who worship idols." Ibn Ezra also says that it refers to the sailors. He explains this is an "intense verb that stresses that the men of the ship were calling out and encouraging one another [in their acts of idolatry]." The sailors did not simply maintain their idolatrous worship. They "zealously guarded" it, clinging to it.

Kimchi explains the use of the word *m'shamrim* to indicate that the sailors maintained their beliefs in false gods even after the events described here. "The men of the ship worshipped many gods. They 'cling to empty folly.'" Kimchi imagines Jonah reflecting, "I knew that after they were saved from their difficulty they would depart from their kindness, from their fear of the Eternal to whom they had cried out and sworn vows. They did not fulfill their vows but rather returned to their worship of many gods. But I did not act like that. Rather in a voice of thanks I worshipped You."

Abarbanel takes a different approach to this verse:

> He [Jonah] does not say this in reference to the sailors and the people of the ship who vowed vows during the storm. Rather when they left the ship they righteously fulfilled their vows as the earlier commentator, Kimchi, explained. And it is not as the sages of blessed memory explained [in Pirke de Rebbi Eliezer] that *chasdam* refers to the acts of kindness that the sailors did in forsaking their gods because they saw the miracles that were done for them. For all these commentators are distant from the meaning of the text. Rather the truth of the matter is that Jonah regretted that he had fled from before the Eternal. And he concluded in his heart to fulfill the commandment of God in the matter of Nineveh. But he was comforted by the statement that the people of Nineveh are "They who cling to empty folly." So even though they will perform repentance in response to his proclamation, they will not remain committed to their repentance. For in a short time they will "forsake their welfare" and return to their evil ways.

Whether it refers to the sailors or to the Ninevites, "They who cling to empty folly" suggests a group of people returning to the wrong path despite ample evidence to avoid it. Many people say: I would serve God if only I saw evidence of God's existence, or evidence of God working in the world. Here both the sailors and the Ninevites, who actually get to see God's power, still do not remain loyal to God. They do not learn the lesson from their experience.

For decades Charles Schultz drew his beloved *Peanuts* comic strip. Every fall during the football season, Schultz would present a strip of Charlie Brown attempting to kick a football held by Lucy, and each time Lucy would pull the football away just as Charlie was about to kick it, causing him to fly up in the air and fall on his back. Charlie never seemed to learn from his experience. Each year Charlie imagined Lucy would be kinder than she actually was.

There is a difference between making a mistake and making the same mistake over and over. Historian Barbara Tuchman in her book *The March of Folly* writes of four moments in history when people clung to the foolish path even when there was ample evidence that they were wrong. She describes the Trojan horse, the British attempting to hold onto the American colonies, six Renaissance popes between 1470 and 1530 whose actions led to the Protestant Reformation, and American policy in Vietnam. In each case repeating unsuccessful policies or actions led to disaster.

In the film *Bridge on the River Kwai* the British colonel, played by Alec Guinness, resists the efforts of the Japanese camp commander to break his will. He wins that "battle," but he inadvertently aids the Japanese war effort by building an excellent British bridge over the river. It is not until the last scenes of the movie when the American, played by William Holden, returns to destroy the bridge that the British colonel realizes his error. As he is about to die, he depresses the plunger, blowing up the bridge. With his last breath he redeems himself.

Kimchi sees the sailors redeeming themselves through their actions after they are saved from the storm. "There is a midrash concerning "Forsaking their righteousness." From this false righteousness they departed. That is to say they departed from their worship of false gods that had been their former mistaken righteousness. Now they had come to realize it was vile." Kimchi continues:

And thus [we read] in Pirke de Rebbi Eliezer, since the sailors when they arrived in Nineveh "saw all the miracles that the Holy One of Praise did with Jonah, they stood up and each man cast away his god into the sea." As it says, "They who cling to empty folly forsake their own welfare." And they returned to Jaffa and went up to Jerusalem and circumcised the flesh of their foreskins.

As it says, "The men feared the Eternal greatly and they offered offerings" (Jonah 1:16). The offering of offerings is the blood of the covenant of circumcision, for it is like the blood of an offering. And each man vowed to bring his wife and children and everything he had to the fear of the Eternal, the God of Jonah. And they made vows and fulfilled them. And concerning them it says, in the thirteenth blessing of the weekday Amidah, "For the proselytes, the proselytes of righteousness."

The sailors focus on their new selves leading new lives rather than looking back at their old selves following their old life paths.

Can we look at our own life situations clearly? Too often we get trapped in the "empty folly" like the British colonel in *Bridge on the River Kwai* or like the people of Troy welcoming the "gift" of the wooden horse left for them by the Greeks. My wife's great-grandfather left Galicia in the early twentieth century with his family on his way to America. They passed through Germany on their way to the ship in Hamburg. A "helpful" relative told them that there was no need for them to continue on to America. He explained that living in Germany would be better than living in America. Later in the 1930s my wife's grandfather had the opportunity to take his family to Argentina. But following his relative's example he decided to remain in Germany. He was sure that this wave of antisemitism would soon conclude just as past waves had subsided. Looking back at the long history of European antisemitism, he could not see how the Nazis would be different.

In recent decades we have witnessed dramatic shifts in the business world due to technological advances. New companies have quickly risen, and some have quickly fallen. Some held on too long to a product that was becoming outdated. In the 1950s and 1960s Kodak seemed like a rock-solid company, a safe investment. Everybody had the latest easy-to-use Kodak camera. Everybody bought film. Many people showed slides of their most recent vacations on Kodak Carousel slide projectors. And then with the advent of electronic images it all quickly changed. Once everyone needed cameras and film, but now hardly anyone is interested. In the 1980s Blockbuster Video rode the wave of the VHS tapes. Virtually every town had a Blockbuster Video store. Thirty years later VHS tapes are as popular as spittoons. Like the *kikayon* plant in chapter 4 of Jonah, "They appeared overnight and perished overnight" (Jonah 4:10). These sophisticated accomplished business leaders of Kodak and Blockbuster continued to look back at past profit statements rather than ahead at the challenges of ever-changing technologies.

Some clear thinkers have seen opportunities created by new technologies. The popularity of professional wrestling rose with the advent of television in the late 1940s and early 1950s. Each TV market had its own World's Champion. In Minnesota, Verne Gagne ruled the wrestling world. As a child I thought he actually was the champion of the world—not, as local sports writer Dick Cullum called him, the champion of the "seven county mosquito control district." From the 1950s through the 1970s, professional wrestling was a regional business, with hubs in many major American cities. Each promoter had his own exclusive territory. With the rise of cable TV in the 1980s, Vince McMahon saw the possibility of converting his father's New York territory into a national and later international business. The WWE has become a global success, and the local regional wrestling territories have just about disappeared.

In our own day-to-day lives, we need to look forward and avoid looking back at the futilities of our past. Too many people act like Lot's wife. They cannot keep their eyes ahead but turn to look back. They focus on a past that is quickly or has already disappeared. Looking back will not literally turn them into pillars of salt, but it may very well keep them stationary as the world around them changes and moves ahead.

31

The Power of the Public Pledge

Which Promises Will We Keep?

"But I, with loud thanksgiving, will sacrifice to You. What I have
vowed I will perform. Deliverance is the Eternal's." —JONAH 2:10

Jonah's prayer has shifted back and forth between descriptions of his
difficult situation and his confidence in God. The prayer concludes
with a verse that contains no reference to the dire straits of Jonah's
current situation in the belly of the fish. Rather it expresses Jonah's
confidence that his life will continue because of God's saving power.
It then concludes with Jonah's pledge to fulfill his vow. But the text
does not tell us what Jonah's vow is. Rashi explains one possible
meaning of the vow. "My [Jonah's] vow is to offer peace and thanksgiving sacrifices for the sake of the salvation that is God's." Kimchi
agrees. He understands Jonah to be saying, "I will thank you with a
voice of thanksgiving from the midst of the congregation." According to Kimchi, Jonah believes that he will join with the community
of worshippers at the Temple in Jerusalem.

Abarbanel takes a different approach. He does not see the vow as
referring to actual offerings:

> He means to say, "I will go to Nineveh with a voice of gratitude and
> I will do the proclaiming you commanded." For that will be like a
> well being and meal offering. For here [in this verse], it is heard it
> will be a good praise offering. And do not think that after I get out
> of here that I will flee a second time like when I went down to Jaffa
> to flee towards Tarshish. In truth it will not be like that. For what
> I have vowed I will perform. And the vow is what he said "with
> loud thanksgiving" that he will go to fulfill the commandment of

the Holy One in Nineveh even though I am frightened and terrified of the destruction of the kingdom of the northern ten tribes at the hands of the Assyrians. I will not worry about it. I will not be anxious because Deliverance is the Eternal's. He will save him in His mercy and draw him close in His loving-kindness.

Malbim agrees with Abarbanel. He imagines Jonah thinking, "What I have vowed I will perform to go to Nineveh. And what I feared is that the king of Assyria will bring evil upon Israel. So to express his concern that God should prevent this from happening, he says, 'For salvation is the Eternal's.' Jonah hopes that the Eternal will redeem Israel from all her difficulties."

While the commentators offer two different opinions about the content of Jonah's vow, all four agree that Jonah takes the vow seriously. Jewish tradition also takes vows seriously. In the Talmud, the sages go to great lengths to find other solutions to a dispute rather than asking the two parties of a dispute to offer a vow. The tractate Baba Metzia begins with a dispute over a found object. Two men walk into the court holding on to a garment. They both claim ownership based on the fact that they found it. If the court asks both men to swear oaths and they do so, one of the men will swear a false oath. To avoid taking steps that would lead to the swearing of a false oath, the sages seek other means to resolve the dispute.

Do we take our vows seriously? Do those around us take them seriously? Our legal system asks all witnesses to swear an oath concerning the honesty of their testimony. Most participants in a trial do not assume that just because the witnesses swore an oath their testimony must be true. We know whom we can count on and who likely will disappoint us. We have reached these conclusions not because of their words but because of their deeds. We see certain friends as trustworthy because they have earned our trust over time, but we can lose trust in a moment. A single misdeed can cause trust earned over many years to disappear in a flash.

I feel that as a rabbi I am earning the trust of my congregants every day. I never say, "Trust me." As a matter of fact, when someone else says, "Trust me," I get suspicious. Truly trustworthy people do not have to ask for trust with words. They demonstrate their trustworthiness through their deeds. I know whom I can count on.

Garrison Keillor in one of his "News from Lake Wobegon" segments describes a grandmother preparing a Thanksgiving dinner as if participating in a competition, even though all the family members have conceded her the championship many years ago. They trust her to make an outstanding feast every year. The people I know I can trust continue to act in a trustworthy manner even though they earned my trust long ago.

We work hard to reach a goal because we believe that other people are paying attention to what we are doing. This is the power of the public pledge. The entire Weight Watchers enterprise stands on this premise. A person stands in front of a group and pledges to lose weight knowing that they will have to return to a future meeting to be weighed in.

Several years ago I spoke on Rosh Hashanah morning about trying new projects. I told the congregation that we should not let age be a barrier to new enterprises. I explained that I was a lifelong fan of folk music, but I lacked musical skill. I was the tone-deaf child asked to sing more softly during school concerts. Nevertheless, despite my lack of natural musical talent, I had decided to learn to play the banjo. As part of the sermon, I publicly declared that if they would return to the synagogue on the evening of Purim, March 17, they would hear me play "A Wicked, Wicked Man" on the banjo. I knew that this public declaration would be enough to propel me forward. The members of the congregation understood that they could trust me to fulfill my public promise because I have earned their trust through years of acting reliably. And it worked. I began banjo lessons that fall and diligently kept at them. And as part of Purim service that spring I played "A Wicked, Wicked Man."

Many movies center on a grand vow. In the classic romance *An*

Affair to Remember, Terry McKay, played by Deborah Kerr, and Nickie Ferrante, played by Cary Grant, fall in love. He aspires to be an artist. There are other obstacles to their love, which they vow to remove over the next twelve months. At the end of that time, they will meet unfettered at the top of the Empire State Building and ideally begin living their lives together. But a year later on her way to meet Nickie, Terry is struck by a car. When she does not arrive to meet him, Nickie believes that Terry has chosen not to keep their date. The accident leaves Terry unable to walk, but Nickie does not know what has happened to her. After a series of twists and turns, Nickie and Terry end up in the same room with one of Nickie's paintings and Terry's wheelchair. Seeing the wheelchair, Nickie now understands why Terry did not make their rendezvous on the top of the Empire State Building. And Terry sees that Nickie has attained success as an artist. They embrace, and she cries out with joy, "If you can paint I can walk!" As the movie ends, the audience is left with the confidence that she will recover from her injuries.

In the film *The Searchers,* John Wayne plays Ethan Edwards, whose niece Debbie, played by Natalie Woods, is kidnaped by the Comanche Indians. Ethan vows not to rest until she is freed. The quest grows complicated, and it takes years, but in the end Ethan returns Debbie to her parents. He fulfills his vow.

In our lives we do not have to free captives with our own hands, but we do each want to be known as a person who should be taken seriously when we make a promise. I want to be able to declare like Jonah, "What I have vowed I will perform." This means that we have to be careful about our promises. We have to avoid making rash promises in the heat of a moment. We should slow down and think before we speak. We should not make a promise because it sounds good at that time or because it expresses what we believe the other person wants to hear. By carefully limiting our "vows" we will much more likely be able to fulfill them.

32

The Hands of God

How Can We Experience the Presence of the Divine?

The Eternal commanded the fish, and it spewed
Jonah out onto dry land. —JONAH 2:11

When people speak about God, too often the conversation moves quickly to the question of belief in God. People either proclaim or deny a belief in God. I don't think that this is the best way to enter a conversation about God. To talk about God we first need to understand what we mean when we say "God." The commentaries about this chapter's verse address a key aspect of understanding God by examining how God works in the world. They begin with the specific question of how God affects the fish that is carrying Jonah in its belly. After looking at this specific question we can expand the conversation to focus on the broader issue of the Divine role in human affairs.

The text says, "The Eternal commanded." Are we to understand that God actually spoke the words that the fish heard? Ibn Ezra suggests that we should read these words in the manner of a metaphor. "The Eternal commanded" means that He compelled the fish to fulfill the Divine wishes. Kimchi says God did not literally have a conversation with the fish. Rather "He revealed His will to the fish so that it would spit him onto dry land."

Abarbanel understands this process a bit differently. He views God as creating the conditions in nature which caused the fish to move landward: "And remember that it is written that when the Holy One saw Jonah's repentance and that he regretted his sin and departed from the path of sin, and that he swore an oath that he would not foolishly flee, then He spoke to the fish. This means to say that He lifted the wind that was blowing to the shore." According to Abarbanel, God indirectly caused the fish to approach the land.

How do we understand God working in the world? We know that some people see God as playing a direct role in the affairs of the world, controlling everything that takes place. Some Sunday morning television preachers hold forth with great confidence that not only does God control our destinies but that they know how and why God shapes human events. Some preachers claimed that Hurricane Katrina struck New Orleans because the "Big Easy" is filled with sin. Rev. John Hagee said, "I believe that New Orleans had a level of sin that was offensive to God, and they are—were—recipients of the judgment of God for that. Our local newspaper carried the story that there was to be a homosexual parade there on the Monday that Katrina came." Hagee believes that God punished New Orleans for promoting Gay Pride.

Some people receive comfort from the concept that God controls everything, but they do not claim to understand God's actions. Rather they say that "God works in mysterious ways." In humility they do not claim to understand God's ways, but they remain confident that the events of the world, including tragic events, are expressions of God's will. I see God as more removed from the events of our everyday lives. I understand that randomness fills our world. When a tornado strikes one side of a street and jumps over the houses on the other side, I see this as a random occurrence rather than an expression of God's will. I see God's presence not in the natural disaster but in our response to it.

In *birkat hamazon*, the blessings after a meal, we praise God for feeding the hungry. In Genesis 3:21 we read of God clothing the naked Adam and Eve. When we feed the hungry and provide clothes to the needy, we become God's partners. All of the volunteers who worked to rebuild New Orleans after Katrina were God's partners.

Early in my career as a congregational rabbi, I received a call from a member who tearfully told me she was about to be evicted from her apartment. She explained that she needed $600 to pay her rent.

I agreed to help her. I decided that I could call six members of the congregation and ask each of them for $100. Asking for money was a new experience for me, but I worked up my courage and made my first call. I told my story, and he quickly told me that he would happy to contribute $100. I thanked him. Then I saw that it would not be as difficult as I had thought it would be. Before I could dial the next fellow on my list, my phone rang. It was the person I had just called. He said, "Rabbi, I am having a good year. You do not have to call anyone else. I can donate the full $600."

More recently I heard that one of our families was about to be evicted from their home because they had fallen far behind on their mortgage. I sent an email to the congregation asking for donations to pay the mortgage for one month to keep this family in their home. Within one day we received sufficient donations to pay the mortgage for two months. I had to actually send a second email to the congregation, thanking the people who had donated and asking people to stop giving. These two experiences taught me that the members of my congregation are ready to be partners with God in supporting those in need. My role was simply to make them aware of the need. We now have an ongoing donative fund at our congregation to provide direct significant aid to families facing this type of challenge.

I like telling the classic story about the wealthy man who enjoyed coming to the synagogue but did not always stay awake. He would always hear the beginning of the rabbi's explanation of the Torah portion, but then he would drift away. On the week of Shabbat Emor he heard the rabbi speak about the twelve loaves of challah to be placed before God. Then he dreamed. When he woke up he knew that God wanted him personally and anonymously to bring the twelve challot to the synagogue before the next Shabbat began. He returned to the synagogue the next Friday carrying twelve challot. When the coast was clear, he snuck into the sanctuary with his twelve challot. He looked around, not sure where to put them. Then he understood. He opened the Ark and put the twelve challot inside, six on one side and six on the other. Before he closed the Ark, he spoke to

God. "Here are the challot you wanted me to bring you. Amen." He left the synagogue and went home.

Sometime later a very poor man entered the synagogue. He stood before the Ark and said, "Master of the universe, we have nothing left to eat. I am turning to you in despair." Then he thought, "Maybe God will hear me more clearly if I open the Ark." He opened the Ark and twelve *challot* fell on him. He concluded that God had answered his prayer. On his way home he stopped in the market, where he traded ten of the *challot* for other types of food.

The next morning the rich man came to the synagogue as usual, but he made it a point to stay awake until the Ark was opened. He wanted to see if God had accepted his *challot*. When the ark was opened, the twelve *challot* were gone!

So every Friday afternoon after that the rich man would put twelve *challot* in the Ark and the poor man would take twelve *challot* out of the Ark. This continued in the same way for months. One Friday the rabbi happened to be in the back of the sanctuary when the rich man brought in the *challot*. He watched in amazement. And then he saw the poor man take the *challot* out of the Ark.

The next morning after services the rabbi introduced the two men to each other and explained what he had seen. The rich man was crushed. "You mean I have not been placing the challot into the hands of God?" The poor man was equally disappointed. "You mean I have not been receiving challot from the hands of God?" The Rabbi took their hands in his. "You have been placing the challot into the hands of God. And you have been receiving challot from the hands of God." The Rabbi said to the rich man, "Your hands are the hands of God." And he said to the poor man, "Your hands are the hands of God."

When we feed the hungry or provide shelter for the homeless, our hands become the hands of God. God works in the world when we respond to God's commanding presence with deeds of loving-kindness.

33

Genuine Forgiveness

Who Deserves a Second Chance?

And the word of the Eternal came to Jonah a second time. —JONAH 3:1

God saved Jonah from drowning because Jonah repented for his sins. But that does not mean that God had to send Jonah to Nineveh. God could easily have sent Jonah home and called another person to be the prophet to the Ninevites. God could have recruited a brand-new prophet for this mission. Or God could have sent a more reliable veteran prophet who had already demonstrated loyalty to God. Perhaps Elijah would have been available for this mission. But instead God gave Jonah a second chance, hoping that Jonah had emerged from the fish a new person.

God put Jonah in exactly the same position that was described in the very first verse of the book of Jonah, expecting that this time he would act differently. The first time God called Jonah, Jonah fled. Now God expects that Jonah will act differently. This is genuine, complete forgiveness. God trusts Jonah.

When those we love disappoint us, are we willing to forgive them in the way that God forgave Jonah? Do we fully trust them? Often when people apologize, they ask for forgiveness and pledge that they will never do it again. Are we willing to give them a second chance?

Athletes caught using performance-enhancing drugs want a second chance. Cheating spouses want a second chance. Dishonest employees want a second chance. Those of us in leadership positions have to distinguish between a firing offense and a lower-level misdeed. We take into consideration intention, scale, and frequency. Some actions will almost always be seen as grounds for dismissal: lying on your resume, selling trade secrets to the competition, or stealing from the company. Does taking a pen home from the office count as stealing? Before answering that question, we must ask a few other questions: How many pens were taken? Was the act intentional or unintentional? One pen ending up in your pocket or purse occasionally is usually acceptable. Taking a case full of pens from the supply closet would generally be seen as theft.

The legal system along with organized sports distinguishes between a first-time offender and a repeat offender. In Jonah's case his misdeed is a one-time event. But it is a major one-time event, a gross neglect of duty.

If I did not come to the synagogue on a Tuesday, people would ask, "I wonder where the rabbi is?" The administrator would say, "He usually tells me when he is not coming in." If then in midafternoon I called from Wrigley Field and apologized for not keeping the staff up to date on my whereabouts, I would be quickly forgiven. But if the Tuesday in question was Rosh Hashanah, or a day on which I was supposed to be officiating at a funeral, I would be guilty of gross neglect of duty. Would the congregation be as forgiving of me as God was of Jonah?

Why does God give Jonah this second chance? Why does God send Jonah to Nineveh? I think that these acts teach us more about God than about Jonah. Jonah does not receive a second chance because Jonah is a "peach of a plum." We have not read anything about Jonah in the Bible itself that shows Jonah to be other than at best an average person. In 4:2 of the book of Jonah, the prophet quotes the book of Exodus 34:6–7 to God: "You are a compassionate and gracious God, slow to anger, abounding in kindness." God forgives Jonah because it is God's nature to forgive. God stands ready to give us the second chances we need, as we all need second chances. We do not find Yom Kippur on Jewish calendars with the words "if necessary." Every year Yom Kippur will be necessary. We do not expect that we will have a year in which we do not sin.

Like many people, I have benefited from receiving second chances. The sixteen-year-old Chalutzim campers I work with at Olin Sang

Ruby Union Institute take a midsummer canoe trip. One summer I was asked to drive a load of ten canoes back to the camp in Oconomowoc, Wisconsin, from the spot where we pulled our canoes out of the Wisconsin River. The camp driver supervised the loading of the canoes on the rack and made sure that they were properly tied to the rack with ropes. Halfway through my journey down I-94 a car started honking at me and then pulled up beside me. The passenger rolled down her window and told me that I had lost a canoe off my rack a half a mile back down the highway.

I pulled off the highway, and sure enough, there were only nine canoes remaining on the rack. I retraced my path. But by the time I got back to the spot where the canoe had fallen off the rack, it was gone. Someone had scavenged the camp's canoe. I rechecked all the ropes and continued back to camp without further incident. I dropped off the canoes and then walked over to the camp director's office to tell him I had lost one of the camp's canoes. I was prepared to offer to pay for the damage I had done, but Jerry would not hear of it. He told me that things like that happen. He thanked me for being willing to help out by hauling the canoes. The next summer they again asked me to haul canoes for the trip. Jerry fully forgave me for losing the canoe and was willing to trust me with exactly the same task at which I had failed. I did notice right away, though, that the camp had invested in proper straps and safety chains to more fully secure the canoes to the rack.

We want everyone we have wronged to give us a second chance to prove ourselves. The question is, are we willing to give a second chance to those who have wronged us? We can hope that those we have wronged will be generous in their forgiveness. But we have control over those who have wronged us. We can choose to be "compassionate and gracious, slow to anger, abounding in kindness" (Exodus 34:6–7). Too many people remember every wrong ever done to them, forgiving and forgetting nothing. At the same time they imagine that their deeds are written on a child's "magic slate" that can be quickly erased simply by lifting the page.

We can find a middle ground between never forgiving or forgetting and the "magic slate" approach. Abarbanel suggests that while God trusted Jonah to deliver the Divine message to Nineveh, he did not honor him with any subsequent prophetic chores. "We do not find any prophesy of his . . . except for these two prophesies on Nineveh. We know that prophesy from him ceased for this reason. And it is appropriate that this happened. For he fled from prophesy, so it was removed from him. His punishment was measure for measure."

At times we learn from our experiences with our friends, co-workers, and relatives what we can expect of them. They may say to us, "I will never do it again." They may be sincere in their declaration. But we would be wise not to accept their statement at face value. As Abarbanel suggests, as God learns that Jonah is not "a good receiver" of prophecy, so we can learn about the strengths and weaknesses of the other people in our lives.

When we avoid expecting those in our lives to exhibit behavior beyond their capacity, we can avoid putting them in situations in which they are bound to fail. In Leviticus 19:14 we read that we should avoid putting a stumbling block before a blind person. We would never literally trip a blind person. But sometimes we might count on a friend or relative to perform a task that we know from bitter experience they cannot do. We can also at times place a stumbling block before ourselves.

Throughout my childhood, I observed my father paying the bills. On Sunday evenings he would take down the cigar box containing the bills and get to work. When my wife and I got married, we had to divide up responsibilities. I thought that I should follow my father's fine example, that I should be responsible for paying the bills in our new family. In a short time I made a mess of it. I neglected to record all of the checks I wrote in the checkbook, and I did not exactly remember to pay all the bills on time. After six months my wife took over our finances. For many years my only monthly financial responsibility was to bring home my paycheck. When the congregation moved to direct deposit, I was relieved even of that small task. Expecting that I would have the same responsibilities in my marriage that my father had in my parents' marriage created a stumbling block for me. Fortunately we recognized and solved the problem before I got us into too much trouble.

At times we can help other people find a new path for their lives that will enable them to avoid the stumbling block over which they have been tripping. Dennis Eckersley began his Major League career as a starting pitcher. In his early years pitching for the Indians and Red Sox he was quite effective. In 1984 the Cubs acquired him in a trade. He pitched well for that year as a starter. But in 1985 and 1986 his performance deteriorated. It seemed that his career had come to an end. The Cubs traded Eckersley to the Oakland A's. The A's manager, Tony La Russa, transformed Eckersley into a relief pitcher. He became the star closer for the A's. He went on to save a total of 390 games.

Baseball managers need to learn who can be a starter and who can be a reliever. We should learn who can handle financial matters and who can handle the food, who will help our elderly relative and who will entertain the youngest generation, who can plan a trip and who can select colors for painting the kitchen, who will do whatever we ask and who will do nothing no matter how many times we ask. We learn whom we can count on to go to Nineveh and who will never get there.

34

Good Guys and Bad Guys

When Can We Accept the Other?

Go at once to Nineveh, that great city, and proclaim to it what I will tell you. . . . Nineveh was an enormously large city. —JONAH 3:2–3

Many people in Chicago love our local sports teams. All of our local teams have "hated" rivals. We support our baseball, basketball, and hockey teams, but most people will agree that Chicago is a football town. We love "Da Bears." And with equal emotion we hate the Green Bay Packers. The two teams have been playing each other since the beginning of the National Football League. New coaches of the Bears understand that their number one job is to beat the Packers.

We like to define ourselves in terms of who we are and who we are not. We want to understand who is on our side and who is on the other side. Verses 2 and 3 in chapter 3 of the book of Jonah describe Nineveh. The commentators disagree about how to understand this description. In 1:2 the text describes Nineveh as "a great city." Here in 3:2 the text again describes Nineveh as a great city. But in 3:3 the text describes Nineveh as "a large city to God." How should we understand the added words, "to God"? Ibn Ezra takes this phrase in 3:3 to mean exactly what it seems to say. Ibn Ezra in his commentary to 1:2 uses this phrase from 3:3 to build his case that the people of Nineveh had a special relationship with the One God of Israel before the events described here.

The other commentators strongly reject Ibn Ezra's approach. Kimchi reads this phrase as a metaphor. He explains that everything the Bible wants to enlarge through description it connects to God in order to enlarge it. This is similar to other biblical examples of descriptions that connect places or events to God in order to intensify the image: "*Kahar'rei eil,* The high mountains" (Psalms 36:7), "*arzeie eil,* Mighty cedars" (Psalms 80:11), "*aish shavhevet'yah,* A blazing flame" (Song of Songs 8:6), and "*mapeil Yah,* Deep gloom" (Jeremiah 2:31). In each case the quoted phrase contains a reference to God that is understood to increase the description rather than to invoke the Deity. Therefore the literal reference to God, *yah* or *eil,* does not appear in the translations.

Abarbanel supports Kimchi's approach:

> To help him [Jonah] understand God's interest in Nineveh, He said to him that because of the size of the city the Holy One of Praise paid attention to it. And that is why the text says that Nineveh was "a great city to God." The intention is not to explain that the people of Nineveh were righteous as was interpreted by our teacher Rabbi Abraham Ibn Ezra. For it was the Land of Assyria. And the nation that dwelled upon it was evil, and they sinned against the Eternal greatly. It came to the attention of God because of its size.

Abarbanel argues that this is similar to other biblical examples of descriptions that connect places or events to God in order to intensify the image. In each case the phrase contains a reference to God that is understood to increase the description rather than to literally invoke the Deity. The text of Jonah uses the term *leilohim* to describe Nineveh: for it was a very large city.

The idea that the people of Nineveh could have had a relationship with the One God of Israel offends Kimchi, Abarbanel, Malbim, and others. They ask how the population of the capital city of our enemy could be in a relationship with our God. This disagreement among the commentators concerning the Ninevites raises the broader question: How do we view the other? I grew up in Minneapolis in the 1960s rooting for the Minnesota Twins. Then I spent four years in Cincinnati in the mid-1970s. While I lived along the banks of the Ohio, I rooted for the Reds. Those were the days of the Big Red Machine, Pete Rose, Joe Morgan, Johnny Bench, and Tony Perez. In 1976 I even got to attend a World Series game. In the summer of 1977 I came to Chicago, a city with two baseball teams. What a treat! That summer I went to the games of both teams. At Wrigley Field I rooted for the Cubs. At old Comiskey Park I rooted for the White Sox. In those days the schedules of the two teams were coordinated so that all summer long, one team was home and one team was on the road. There was a game in town every day, and I was in baseball heaven.

Native Chicagoans told me that I had it all wrong. They explained to me that I had to choose the Cubs or the Sox. I had seen evidence of this divide. At the Sox games I saw Sox fans wearing T-shirts that read, "My favorite team is the Sox. My second favorite team is whoever is playing the Cubs." We tend to be drawn into demonizing the other. During World War II, American propaganda portrayed the Japanese as a foreign, grotesque, and uncivilized enemy. Posters often pictured the Japanese soldiers and leaders as resembling rats. Often parodies of wartime leader Hideki Tojo portrayed him with grotesquely exaggerated features such as elongated fangs.

Many people fall into the trap of dividing the world into two groups: our enemies and our friends, the good guys and the bad guys. This division may be good fun when talking about sports. But it can cause deep harm when applied to religion and world affairs.

When a new conflict appears on the world stage, people want to know the good guys from the bad guys. Life is more complicated than that. We need to probe the subtleties and nuances of world events and the events of our everyday lives. Too many people do not take the time to gain an in-depth understanding of world events. I hear people hold forth with great confidence on events that they do not understand. They tend to view societies as monolithic, when in truth there exist many factions within the society in question. Sometimes I hear Jews speak about Christians as if they were a cohesive group of believers who share identical values and beliefs. In truth the term *Christian* describes a broad range of people with contrasting beliefs and practices.

Also people with whom we disagree do not need to be considered our enemies. During the National Hockey League's playoffs, the teams go at each other violently with their bodies and with their sticks. At the conclusion of every series, no matter how violent the games have been, the two teams line up and shake hands. These handshakes express the players' respect for the game of hockey and their respect for each other as worthy participants.

Many of the commentators strongly object to Abraham Ibn Ezra's understanding of the phrase "a large city to God" to indicate that God had a special relationship with the people of Nineveh; after all, the Assyrians were our enemy. In his commentary Ibn Ezra writes about the religion of the Ninevites, but I suspect that he really intends to communicate his appreciation of other religions of his own time. He argues that one does not have to be Jewish to have a proper relationship with the One God.

The other whom we do not yet understand does not have to be evil. One can be completely different from us and still be in a relationship with God. The Torah tells us, "Love your neighbor as yourself." The challenge often for us lies in being able to see those we do not know or understand as our neighbors.

35

Hineini

How Do We Respond When Called?

> Jonah went at once to Nineveh, in accordance with
> the Eternal's command. Nineveh was an enormously
> large city, a three-day walk. —JONAH 3:3

The biblical text does not record Jonah saying a word in response to
God's renewed call to go to Nineveh. Jonah silently goes about his
business. We do not get a lot of specific details about his journey.
Did he walk to Nineveh by himself? Or did he join a camel caravan
like the one that took Joseph to Egypt? How long did it take Jonah
to get from the seashore to Nineveh? Often stories in the Bible leave
us wanting to know more. The only detail of the journey that the
text does provide is the mention of "a three-day walk" at the conclusion of the verse.

It is not clear what the phrase "a three-day walk" describes. Some
people take it to mean that Jonah walked three days from where the
fish deposited him on dry land to reach Nineveh. The commentators,
who are familiar with the geography of the Middle East, understand
that no one could walk the hundreds of miles from the Mediterra-
nean coast to Nineveh in three days. Even with camels it would take
a few weeks to cross from the sea to Nineveh.

Some people understand this phrase to mean that it took three
days to walk across the city of Nineveh. That would be unbelievably
large even by modern standards. A reasonably healthy person could
easily walk across the entire thirty-five-mile-wide Chicago metropoli-
tan area in two days. Certainly ancient Nineveh was much smaller
than modern Chicago! Ibn Ezra explains that this does not describe
the diameter of the city but rather the circumference of the entire

district. It would take three days to walk around the district. The one-day walk in verse 4 should not be understood as walking straight into the city, for he would emerge from the other side before the day was done. Ibn Ezra continues that it could mean that he walked one day from one side to the other, [speaking as he went to the Ninevites he encountered, or it could mean] that when he walked [to Nineveh] to proclaim what God had told him, it would take one day to walk there.

Abarbanel disagrees with Ibn Ezra. "And according to the plain meaning of the text Rabbi Abraham Ibn Ezra wrote that it was a three-day walk around the province and a one-day walk across. And his words are not correct. For the text of verse 4 says, 'Jonah began to enter the city the distance of a one-day walk.' This teaches that he did not cross the entire way, for he had stopped. Therefore, we can see that from city gate to city gate it is three days." Both commentators seek to make sense out of an incomplete phrase. Each adds to the actual biblical text to create a full image.

When I read the phrase "three-day walk" in this verse, I hear an echo of an earlier Bible story. In Genesis 22 God calls Abraham to offer his son Isaac as a sacrifice. Abraham and Isaac's journey from their home to Mount Moriah takes three days, as does Jonah's walk in our story. The length of their journey was similar, but the stories we tell about these two men are very different. While we speak of Abraham as a man of faith, we see Jonah as a man of fear.

God first calls Abraham in Genesis 12:1 and says to him, "Go forth from your native land and from your father's house." Abraham responds by following God's instructions. He gets up and goes; he does not ask God any questions. He does not ask God, why me? He does not ask God about the quality of this new land or about the people who dwell there. God calls Abraham, and he responds by going. The first time God calls Jonah, Jonah flees. He runs away in the opposite direction. God wants him to go east to Nineveh, but he runs west to Jaffa. Here in Jonah 3:3 God gives Jonah a second chance, and the reluctant prophet follows Abraham's example. He gets up and he goes.

In Genesis 22:1 God calls to Abraham, and Abraham responds, *"Hineini,"* or "here I am." In our story in verse 2, God calls Jonah to go to Nineveh. Jonah does not say, *"Hineini."* Jonah never says, *"Hineini."* Jonah does not say a word in response to either of God's calls to go to Nineveh. The first time he flees, and this time he goes, but he does not speak. Often people in the Hebrew Bible respond to a call by saying, *"Hineini,"* but not Jonah.

I teach Introduction to the Bible at Elmhurst College. Since Elmhurst is affiliated with the United Church of Christ, I teach Bible as defined by Christians. I teach the Hebrew text and Christian scripture, the Torah, Prophets, and Writings, and also the Four Gospels and Paul's Epistles. So students can come to Elmhurst College and have a rabbi teach them the Gospels. This says a great deal about progress in Jewish–Christian relations in our country. My students at Elmhurst College are, of course, not Hebrew speakers. We read the Bible in English. But there is one Hebrew word I make the students learn: *hineini.* A simple translation would be, "Here I am." The first year I taught this word, one student made use of it when I took attendance. I called his name and rather than saying, "Here" he proudly called out, *"Hineini."*

While my Elmhurst College student enjoyed using this newly acquired Hebrew vocabulary to answer my roll call, the word *hineini* expresses a more profound message. When I say this word, I do more than simply describe my geographic location. I proclaim my presence. I am really here. I am fully present. I am here for you. When I say, *"Hineini,"* I proclaim this is me and I am here for you.

Hineini is a key word in the binding of Isaac story, appearing three times. Abraham recites it in his initial response to God's call; he tells God, "I am ready to do as you ask." A bit later as Abraham and Isaac climb the mountain, Isaac calls to his father in a questioning voice, *"Avi,* my father?" Abraham reassures his son by responding, *"Hineini b'ni,* Here I am, my son." Abraham uses this word to express to Isaac that he is there to protect him. At the dramatic high point of the story as Abraham stands over the bound Isaac with a knife in his hand, he hears a voice from above call out, "Abraham, Abraham." Abraham responds to God, "*Hineini.*" Abraham uses *hineini* to say, "I am here and I am confident I will not have to kill my son."

This word appears elsewhere in the Hebrew Bible. When God calls to Moses at the burning bush, Moses responds to God by saying, "*Hineini*" (Exodus 3:4). Moses expresses the same confidence in God that Abraham expressed. Speaking to the Israelites in exile in Babylonia, the prophet Isaiah assures them that when they turn back to God, God will respond to them by saying, "*Hineini*" (Isaiah 58:9). Isaiah explains that as Abraham and Moses were fully present when God called them, so God will be fully present when called upon by the Israelites.

I believe that Jonah never recites this key declaration of presence, *hineini,* because he is never as fully present to God as Abraham and Moses were. Jonah goes to Nineveh to fulfill his mission, but he has not fully committed himself to God's cause. He still harbors doubts. We will see these doubts emerge in chapter 4 of Jonah's story. He will not rejoice in God's merciful response to the repentance of the Ninevites. And there we will see the ways in which Jonah expresses his resentment.

Hineini is an important word for my Elmhurst College students to know and a word for my students to say. In class we practice saying *hineini* out loud. It should be an important word for us as well. When we hear ourselves called, we should also be able to respond *hineini,* that we are fully present. When people tell stories about us, they should tell tales of a person who hears the call and responds, *hineini.*

36

The Freedom to Choose

Can We Respond to a Warning?

> And Jonah started out and made his way into the city the
> distance of one day's walk and proclaimed, "Forty days
> more, and Nineveh will be overturned." —JONAH 3:4

Let's look closely at the wording of Jonah's proclamation. The more
literary NJPS translation renders the final word, *nehpachet,* as "overthrown." A more literal translation of *nehpachet* is "overturned."
Jonah does not say, "In forty days Nineveh will be destroyed." He
says overturned rather than destroyed. And he does not couch his
proclamation in if/then language. Jonah does not say to the Ninevites,
"If you do not repent, Nineveh will be overturned in forty days." He
does not explicitly indicate to the Ninevites that they could escape
destruction by changing their lives.

Rashi points out the significance of Jonah's use of the ambigu-
ous term *overturned.* Jonah warns the people that Nineveh will be
destroyed. The text does not simply use the term *destroyed* because
overturned can be used in two different ways, bad and good. If they do
not repent, then Nineveh will be overturned. If they do repent, then
that which was proclaimed concerning the people of Nineveh will
be overturned, for they turned over from bad to good and repented.

Abarbanel more fully develops the interpretation suggested by
Rashi. Why doesn't Jonah say, "If you do not repent, Nineveh will
be overturned in forty days"?

> What appears to me to answer the first question is that the con-
> dition in this designation [can be understood] in two ways. The
> first is the straightforward approach, that in forty days Nineveh

will be overturned [one way or another]. And this is proven now that if the residents turn in repentance, there will be overturning through their deeds of their direction from evil to good, from misdeeds to the most righteous of the righteous. And according to the approach which says, "And Nineveh will be overturned, *V'nineveh nehpachet*," which follows from the language of a man who is overturned following "My heart has turned over within me, *nehpach libi b'kirbi*" (Lamentations 1:20). This verse from Lamentations proves that the Bible uses the term *nehpachet* to refer to a profound change in human beings. And if they do not repent, there will be destruction like that of Sodom and Gomorrah. And this approach is sustained from all sides, since the word *nehpachet* includes both meanings, overturned and destroyed. And Hashem did not command the prophet to proclaim, "And Nineveh will be destroyed like Sodom and Gomorrah." Rather, God commanded Jonah to say *nehpachet*, since God simply wants to show that in forty days it will be *nehpachet*. If it will be in their eyes to perform repentance and overturn their deeds in turning to God, then this decree will be cancelled.

Three times in the Hebrew Bible, God announces the intention to destroy populations because of the evil of the inhabitants' behavior: the generation of Noah, the cities of Sodom and Gomorrah, and the residents of Nineveh. Only the Ninevites receive a direct verbal warning, which serves no purpose except to give them a chance to repent. Only the Ninevites repent and avoid destruction, and Jonah's prophecy comes true. Nineveh is indeed overturned—not by Divine destruction but by the repentance of the people of Nineveh. They turn over a new leaf.

Why do the Ninevites pay attention to this prophet from a foreign land? Ibn Ezra explains that the Ninevites had heard stories about Jonah before he ever set foot in the Assyrian capital. Ibn Ezra writes: "Rabbi Joshua said that the men of the ship went to Nineveh and told them the story of Jonah and therefore they had faith in the Eternal." According to Ibn Ezra, Jonah reacts positively to this second call from God because he knows that when he arrives in Nineveh, he will not be seen as an unknown Israelite. Rather, he will be a person whose reputation precedes him. He can expect that the people of Nineveh will respond to his words, having already heard the testimony of the sailors.

Can we learn from the example of the Ninevites? Can we turn our lives around when we get warnings? We get implicit and explicit warnings: from our own bodies warning us of problems and from our doctors warning us about unhealthy habits. In relationships we also get implicit and explicit warnings.

Over the years I have met with married couples whose marriages were crumbling. Recently I met with a couple already past the crisis. I sensed that the wife had told her husband she wanted a divorce and he had responded with "Let's try to get help." The wife had agreed to come see me to placate her soon to be ex-husband but had no interest in repairing their relationship. My task became helping the husband come to grips with the reality that the marriage was over. I listened to the wife explain what had brought them to this moment of no return. The husband expressed a readiness to change, but it was too late. If the first time his wife had pointed out the problem, he had said what he was now saying, their marriage could have continued on. But he ignored the words of warning. And now his life was indeed overturned.

A few years ago during a trip to Israel I had an unexpected learning experience at Masada. We woke early in the morning to climb up Masada via the Roman ramp. I carefully watched my step going up the ramp. After a thorough tour of the top of Masada, we walked down the Snake Path. Again I walked carefully. After we all safely reached the bottom we stopped in the visitors' center before boarding our bus. As I stood waiting, a very large fellow hurried out, not looking where he was going. He crashed into me, and I fell flat on my face. For a moment I was stunned. I did not understand what had happened. I was bleeding from my nose and lip.

People rushed over to help me to the first aid station. A medic washed and bandaged me. I looked awful, but I did not need stiches. I got a warning that day—to walk defensively. I now pay attention to how the people around me are walking, and I take note of those walking without paying attention to where they are going. During the Cold War, America placed radar stations in northern Canada as an early warning system to track incoming Soviet missiles. I practice defensive walking as my own early warning system.

Too often we choose to ignore the warnings until it is too late. We wait until our health can no longer be regained. We delay until our relationships can no longer be repaired. Too often we ignore the dangers as they approach us. God sent Jonah to warn the Ninevites. They responded to his warning, and it saved their lives. We need to pay attention to warnings we receive.

37

Who, What, Why, and When

Can We Ask the Probing Questions?

The people of Nineveh believed God. —JONAH 3:5

During the summer before our senior year in high school, my friend Larry, the editor of the school paper, recruited me to fill an open spot on the paper's staff as assistant business manager. My task would be to arrange ads for the paper from local merchants.

All the other members of the paper's staff had already taken the required Introduction to Journalism course, and to qualify for the post I had to agree to take the course myself that fall. I took it so I could work with my friends on the paper, not because I had any genuine interest in journalism. But as the year went on, I actually learned how to write a news story. Miss Steinberg taught me how to ask the probing questions and how to write a lead paragraph.

Milwaukee civil rights leader Father James Groppi came to speak at University of Minnesota. I suggested to Miss Steinberg that I go to the lecture and write an article for our paper. This was well beyond the scope of my responsibility as assistant business manager, but she agreed and said she would not commit to publishing it until she read it. My article passed her scrutiny. She was satisfied that I had asked Father Groppi the correct questions. The paper published my article, and it won a high school journalism award.

The probing questions of journalists—what, why, and who—are exactly the questions which the commentators raise concerning the first phrase of this chapter's verse.

What did the Ninevites believe?

Ibn Ezra explains that the first phrase of our verse is similar to another biblical verse: "And the nation believed" (Exodus 4:31). There, in the book of Exodus, the people of Israel responded to Moses and believed. Here the people of Nineveh respond to Jonah and believe. Ibn Ezra explains that what is reported here is not an abstract theological statement that the Ninevites believed in the existence of the God of Israel. Rather they believed that "the word of God" of Israel as spoken by Jonah was true. They believed that Nineveh was about to be destroyed because they recognized Jonah as an authentic representative of God.

Kimchi explains why the Ninevites respond so dramatically to Jonah's words: "For the men of the ship were in the city and they gave testimony concerning him." They told the story of the storm and admitted that they had thrown him into the sea. They said, "And all of our witnessing is exactly as it happened." Therefore the Ninevites believed in his prophecy and repented.

Malbim offers an alternative view: "And it is notable that they believed immediately and they did not ask for a sign or a miracle. And immediately they began to pray through the means that they put on sackcloth to fast and be humble. And the nation was not roused to repentance because it did not occur to them that they were sinners because Jonah had not informed them of this. This is how it appears to me." Kimchi thinks the Ninevites believed Jonah's words because of evidence, while Malbim thinks they accepted his words without question and opened their eyes so that they, for the first time, saw clearly the evil of their ways.

In whom did the Ninevites believe?

Abarbanel distinguishes between belief in God and belief in Jonah:

Jonah explains to them this proclamation concerning their sins in general and in detail about the violence of their hands, their deeds. And they turned to Hashem. And God had mercy. . . . They accepted the words of Jonah to become good and proper from his mouth. Thus it says, "And the people of Nineveh believed in God." It does not say that they believed in Jonah or that the king of Nineveh called him to appear at the palace or spoke to him about this matter. Rather it says that they believed in God, that it was in His hands to do all of this [the destruction of Nineveh]. And that He loves the righteous and He hates violence. They are awoken by the words of Jonah to perform their repentance.

Rarely does the Hebrew Bible speak of people having faith in God; rather, it focuses on the questions of how people act rather than on what they believe. Christians easily speak of faith; it appears hundreds of times in Christian scripture. Paul in his epistles stresses faith in Jesus as the key to salvation. "For we hold that one is justified by faith apart from works of the law" (Romans 3:28). Paul often speaks of Christians as believers (1 Corinthians 6:5). People continue to speak of the Christian faith. Christians see themselves as being part of a faith community.

The Christian emphasis on faith has moved Jews to be wary of the term. In the rabbinic period there were distinctions between ritual practice in the Land of Israel and those in Babylon. The rabbis of Babylonia established the book of Jonah as the *haftarah* on Yom Kippur afternoon because of its expression of God's forgiveness of Jonah and of the Ninevites. And it is read to this day by all Jewish communities. But in the Land of Israel during the rabbinic period, Jonah was not recited as the *haftarah* on Yom Kippur, because the local sages saw it as "too Christian"—that faith was everything, and that all the Ninevites had to do to be saved from destruction was to have faith. According to Professor Avigdor Shinan of the Hebrew University, these sages objected to the reading of Jonah on Yom Kippur because the rabbis of the Land of Israel took great pains to distinguish themselves from emerging Christianity. The Jews of the Land of Israel lived in the presence of emerging Christianity that was not present in Babylonia.

Let's return to the questions of a journalist. What did the Ninevites believe as a result of Jonah's brief prophecy? They realized that they would be destroyed as the consequence of their deeds. Why did the Ninevites believe Jonah? The timing of his message was key.

They must have already known on some level that their deeds were unacceptable. Often people continue on a path they know is wrong simply because no one has told them to stop. They believe they are getting away with it. Drinkers believe that nothing negative results from their drinking until people close to them gather together for an intervention. Jonah's prophecy serves as an intervention for the Ninevites. As Malbim suggested above, until Jonah spoke up, no one had uttered a word of rebuke to them.

We can also ask the journalists' questions about our own ideas concerning God. When I say I believe in God: What do I mean? Why do I believe? In whom do I believe?

I do not hold to a magical view of God who will come to the rescue of those in need. As a child I loved Mighty Mouse cartoons. These cartoons told the stories of a mouse with the strength of Superman swooping in to assist those in need. The theme song proclaimed, "Here I come to save the day; that means that Mighty Mouse is on the way." As an adult I understand that God does not operate like a cartoon superhero. God does not swoop in to save a person from drowning or to cure a person's malignant cancer. For me, God does not operate in the world as an independent entity. Rather I see God as the foundation of the world.

I believe in God as a source of wisdom, strength, and courage. I believe in God as the ground of ethics. I need God in my life. I need a center, a foundation. I believe in God and in humanity. Each day I see evidence of the corrupted evil ways men and women can act. But I also see modest acts of loving-kindness. And I see people dedicate themselves to public causes to change the world.

Whom does God call? God calls us to act in the world. Near the end of the *Aleinu* prayer we proclaim our role "to repair the world under the sovereignty of God." We repair the world by fighting for justice and by treating people we encounter every day with love and respect.

38

Letting the Current Carry Me

How Do We Respond to Reality?

They proclaimed a fast, and great and small alike put on
sackcloth. When the news reached the king of Nineveh,
he rose from his throne, took off his robe from upon him,
put on sackcloth, and sat in ashes. —JONAH 3:5–6

Some years ago our extended family gathered in New Mexico to celebrate my mother's birthday. One morning some of us went white-
water rafting on the Rio Grande. Before we climbed into our rafts,
Abel, our guide, gave us a safety orientation. He explained that if
you fall out of your raft, you should not try to stand up. If you do so,
your feet will get stuck among the rocks, and the current will knock
you over, causing injuries or worse. Abel told us that if you do fall
out, just lean back and float, let the current carry you downstream.
He said that as the current is carrying the raft downstream, float
toward the raft and those still aboard will pull you back in. He even
explained how someone in the raft could get the proper leverage to
pull a person from the river back into the raft.

We climbed into the raft; I sat in the front. During the trip our raft
hit a big rock. The raft stopped, but I did not: I fell out. Suddenly I
was in the river. I followed Abel's instructions, and I floated. My life
jacket held me up, and I felt just fine. Slowly I moved back toward the
raft. Abel told my brother that he would be the one to pull me back
into the raft. Ken jokingly said to Abel, "Am I my brother's keeper?"
But then he got on his knees and grabbed me by the straps of my
lifejacket. Following Abel's instructions, he then fell backwards.
That motion pulled me back into the boat. I landed on top of him.
I did just fine in the river because I did not resist the current. I let

the current carry me. The leader who knows how to bend with the current of public opinion can be carried forward. The clever leader keeps up with the people.

In the Jonah story it appears that the people had already begun to repent before the king even heard what was going on in the city. The population of Nineveh did not wait for the king to declare a fast; they took their own initiative. And the king took his cue from the people's response.

Our text could have followed a different narrative line. It could have followed the model of Moses and Aaron directly confronting Pharaoh, beginning in Exodus 5:1. Moses and Aaron stood before the ruler of Egypt and proclaimed, "Let my people go." Jonah could have appeared before the king of Nineveh to proclaim the city's fate. But instead Jonah speaks in an unidentified public location in the midst of the people. The message reaches the king secondhand. In the Exodus text, Pharaoh was the target of the Eternal's words. Here the Eternal speaks through Jonah to the entire population of Nineveh.

Some commentators raise questions about which came first, the king's proclamation, described in verse 6, or the people's repentance, in verse 5. The sequence of the verses certainly suggests that the people acted before the king spoke.

Some commentators, such as Ibn Ezra, argue that the sequence of the verses does not reflect the sequence of events. He suggests that the phrase "And the word reached" [from verse 6] is before "the people put on sackcloth." Ibn Ezra explains that the sequence of the verses in this section does not match the sequence of events as they actually took place. The acts of repentance described in the second half of verse 5 did not take place until after the king's response described in verses 6 through 9. According to Ibn Ezra, the people put on sackcloth and fasted in response to the king's decree. Kimchi, however, argues that "before the warning of the king, they made repentance on their own. They humbled themselves and put on sackcloth." The people act before the king issues a royal proclamation. The text describes an immediate grassroots response to Jonah's words.

Fasting is a standard method for people in the Hebrew Bible to use when they seek God's intervention. In 2 Samuel 12:16 King David wants God to heal his gravely ill child. "David fasted." In Ezra 8:23 Ezra wants God to protect the people on their journey from Babylonia back to Jerusalem, "So we fasted and besought our God," and 2 Chronicles tells of King Jehosaphat of Judah's fear of an attack by the Moabites and the Ammonites. In 20:3 he turns to God. "Then Jehosaphat was afraid; he decided to resort to the Eternal and proclaimed a fast for all Judah."

Sackcloth and ashes often accompanied fasting back then. The prophet Isaiah criticizes the people of his time who fast seeking God's forgiveness but do not forsake their evil ways. He asks on God's behalf, "Is the fast that I desire a day for men to starve their bodies? Is it bowing the head like a bulrush and lying in sackcloth and ashes?" (Isaiah 58:5).

The king of Nineveh could have stubbornly refused to follow the lead of his people. He could have declared in a Nixonian fashion, "I am the king." But instead he acts with humility and wisdom. The text literally says that the king "removed his glory." Rashi understands that it refers to "his precious clothing," for in the last portion of the verse we read that the king puts on sackcloth. Kimchi elaborates, "The robe of royalty he was wearing." And Targum Yonaton renders it "clothing of honor." He takes off his royal garments. He follows the example of the people and puts on sackcloth and then goes one step further and sits in ashes.

We can learn from the example of the king of Nineveh. We can pay attention to what is going on around us. "When the winds of changes shift" (Bob Dylan), we can adjust. We are all creatures of the era in which we came of age. I am a son of the sixties. My mother is a child of the Great Depression. But we do not need to stay locked in the times of our origin. While I may still listen to the same music of my teenage years, my sense of the world around me has changed over time and continues to change.

As the leader of a congregation I have learned to ask our members to tell me their stories. We have applied the tools of community organizing to our congregation. We have drawn on the efforts of the Union for Reform Judaism's Just Congregation project and on the experience of DuPage United, our local community-organizing group. We have, in a systematic manner, conducted a long series of one-on-one conversations with our members. The first step in every conversation is for each of the two people to tell the other his or her story, so we can learn more about the person and their concerns. We have then brought together people with similar concerns and interests. A number of projects for our congregation have grown out of these one-on-one conversations.

I remember the lessons I learned from Abel. I continue to apply them to my life. When I fall off the "raft," I do not try to stand up. I let the current carry me back. I pay attention to what is going on around me. I listen to what others have to say. We should not let our egos get in the way of learning from everybody we encounter. As Ben Zoma teaches, "Who is wise? The one who learns from all people" (Pirke Avot 4:1). I apply this wisdom to my work as a rabbi in our congregation and to my life with my family.

39

Telling Tall Tales

How Do We Sort Out the Truth?

And he had the word cried through Nineveh: "By decree of the king and his nobles: No man or beast—of flock or herd—shall taste anything! They shall not graze, and they shall not drink water!" —JONAH 3:7

When I tell stories, I like to use exaggeration to bring in some humor. If I am not sure that my listeners understand that I am kidding, I will increase the level of exaggeration so that people know not to take it seriously. I notice that other people will tip off their humorous intent by saying, "Seriously" or "I'm not kidding." In this verse we will see another example of exaggeration in the book of Jonah.

The verse begins with a difficult phrase. As we have seen in earlier chapters, the English translation may mask the difficulties of the original Hebrew. Translators have to unravel the puzzling word choices of the author in order to present a cogent English version of the text. In Hebrew the verse begins, "*Vayazeik, vayomair.*" *Vayomair* is a word used throughout the Hebrew Bible to mean "he said." The general meaning of the root of *vayazeik* is "cry out." Our verse uses a *hifil* verb form expressing causation. Rashi explains that the king did not himself cry out the proclamation to the Ninevites but rather he commanded that it be publicly proclaimed. Kimchi adds, "He caused an announcement to be made in the city concerning the repentance. And even though the people were already enlightened concerning God." As we saw in the previous verse, the king is trying to catch up with the general population. The king and his courtiers proclaim a fast that the people have already begun. They make official government policy out of something that is already happening.

The curious part of this verse comes in the broad application of the order to fast. Not only will all the people of Nineveh fast but the animals will fast as well. Kimchi writes that "this added the contrition of the animals to the contrition of the people." Abarbanel explains the king proclaimed "that the people and the animals will not eat and will not drink." The people have to repent and fast because they have sinned. Why do the animals have to repent and fast? Abarbanel answers, "And this order applies to the animals even though they do not possess discernment because the eyes of every human being are on them. [The people can learn from the animals.] And the Holy One will provide their food in its time. So now the cattle in the pens of the city will cry out before Him, so that He will have mercy upon them."

We do not usually think of contrition as being an act of animals. We can say, "Bad dog!" to a pet that has chewed on the furniture. But does the dog have to express contrition? Certainly other less intellectually advanced animals do not express contrition. I spend three and a half weeks every summer in Wisconsin, "America's Dairyland." I have never seen a contrite cow.

The fasting animals stand out as a prime example of exaggeration in the book of Jonah. We see exaggeration throughout this short book. The storm that attacks the ship is huge. The fish that swallows Jonah is large enough to swallow a man whole. Jonah's ability to remain alive in the belly of the fish for three days challenges reality. The text exaggerates the size of Nineveh, describing it as larger than a modern city. The complete repentance of the entire population of Nineveh seems to be an exaggeration as well. No population of any city ever agrees 100 percent on anything.

I see the book of Jonah as a tall tale. We are familiar with American tall tales. Some have a basis in historic fact, whereas others are entirely fictional. American children learn that John Henry was a steel driving man. Pecos Bill could lasso a tornado. Mike Fink was the king of the keelboats. As a Minnesota boy, my favorite was Paul Bunyan and Babe the Blue Ox. Paul Bunyan was a legendary north woods lumberjack who could eat fifty pancakes at a time. To grease the gigantic cook stove in the loggers' camp, Paul would skate on the stove with hams strapped to his feet. Paul cut down an enormous number of trees wherever he went. Babe was Paul's sidekick. Babe's footstep throughout Minnesota's north woods became lakes, 10,000 lakes to be precise. Paul Bunyan fills Minnesota culture. During the 1960s, I listened to Minneapolis's Top 40 rock and roll station, WDGY. In the evenings their disc jockey was Tall Paul Bunyan.

When I was a child my family took a summer fishing vacation at Leech Lake in northern Minnesota. My parents told me that on our way north we were going to see Paul Bunyan and Babe the Blue Ox. I was quite disappointed when we got to town. What we saw were statues, not an actual lumberjack and giant ox. Later I learned that DJ Tall Paul Bunyan was actually named Tom Campbell.

When we come of age we begin to learn that the magical beliefs of our childhood are not actually true. I got over learning that Paul Bunyan and Babe the Blue Ox were not real. I recovered from learning that radio personalities use stage names. I was even able to recover from the shock of discovering that Roy Rogers was not actually "the King of the Cowboys."

There are many biblical stories that I do not take literally. I will easily agree that the Garden of Eden, Noah's Ark, and the Tower of Babel have no basis in fact. However, I know that Assyrian sources attest to King Hezekiah ruling in Judah. The Assyrian sources and the book of Kings tell similar stories of the Assyrian siege of Jerusalem. So I accept Hezekiah as real. What about the Bible characters after Noah and before Hezekiah? I see those closer in time to Hezekiah more likely to be historically true and those closer to Noah more likely to be legendary. Does this position stop me from telling the stories of the book of Genesis to young children? On Passover will I stop proclaiming that "God took us out of Egypt with a mighty hand and outstretched arm?" (Haggadah). No.

Stories play a key role in the life of the child. The challenge is to help the teen transitioning into adulthood to learn to read the stories in a more sophisticated way. I fear that many people who reject religion as adults never made this transition from a juvenile to an adult manner of reading the stories and learning the truths. Young children view their parents as all-knowing and as all-powerful. In each person's life a time comes when we learn that parents are human beings who are not always right and not all-powerful.

In healthy families teens can make this transition and develop strong adult-adult connections with their parents. But we know that in some families this does not happen. Kids get stuck in the teenage phase of life and fail to launch. They remain combative teenagers well into their adult years. I see this same dynamic in the distance some people maintain from religious life. They have failed to launch. They remain stuck in an adolescent struggle with God. Relying on a child's concept of God, they do not understand how God could allow tragedies in their lives or in the larger world to occur.

Our verse speaks of the "counsel of the king and his nobles." The term in the original Hebrew is *ta'am*. Ibn Ezra explains that this word comes "from his advice, his knowledge, and his wisdom. And this is similar to 'in changing his discernment.'" Psalms 34:1 refers to an incident in 1 Samuel 21:14f in which David feigns madness during his flight from Saul. David pretends to be mad so that King Achish of the Philistine city of Gath will give him sanctuary. David changes his discernment to fit the circumstance.

As adults we have to change our discernment to approach these religious questions in a mature and sophisticated manner. As we have resolved our adolescent struggles with our parents, we should resolve our adolescent struggle with God. We should be open to more subtle ways of understanding God's role in our lives. God does not control us. God calls to us through the words of our sacred texts and the examples of the righteous people around us.

40

Controlling Our Inclinations

Can We Change Our Evil Ways?

"They shall be covered with sackcloth—man and beast—and
shall cry mightily to God. Let everyone turn back from his evil
ways and from the injustice of which he is guilty" —JONAH 3:8

Major musical pieces like a Beethoven symphony often have a theme
that runs throughout the piece. The recurring theme in the book
of Jonah is the possibility of change. Jonah's attitude toward God
changed while he was in the belly of the big fish. The sailors on
the ship became worshippers of the One God of Israel in response
to being saved from the storm. To understand how the Ninevites
change, we need to look a bit more closely at the extent of their evil
and the nature of their repentance.

This verse begins with a continuation of the use of exaggeration
in storytelling. In the last verse we learned that the animals fasted.
Here we learn that not only did these pious animals fast but they also
wore sackcloth. In the second phrase of this verse, they cry mightily
out to God. But who cried mightily to God? At the beginning of the
sentence we read of people and animals. From the structure of the
sentence one might conclude that the people and the animals called
out to God. Ibn Ezra makes it clear that this second clause refers to
a person: "Whether he is the son of knowledge rational or he is one
who knows he did wrong."

The last phrase of this verse uses the Hebrew word *chamas*, violence, translated above as "evil ways." This is the first time that *chamas*
appears in the book of Jonah. *Chamas* is the word that the Hebrew
Bible uses to describe the generation of Noah and the population
of Sodom. By using *chamas* here, the Bible puts the sins of the Nin-

evites in the same category as those of the generation of Noah and the people of Sodom.

Kimchi explains: "This [sin of violence] is equal to all of them [all the other sins]. And for this sin the proclamation was issued." Abarbanel agrees concerning the seriousness of the sin of violence. "And the king also commanded that the people should have no doubt about the acts of fasting and the wearing of sackcloth that they do. But rather this sinful people will strongly call out to God. And repent of the violence of their hands. Which is the central issue."

Rashi suggests that the Ninevites were so violent that they even used violence in their appeal to God as described in this verse. He provides an imaginative reading of *mightily*. Most readers take it to describe the intensity of the appeal of the Ninevites, but Rashi understands *mightily* to mean "with might." Rashi suggests that they used an act of might to state their case to God. "The men of Nineveh took hostage the mothers, separately, and the children, separately. They said before the Master of the Universe, 'If you do not show us mercy, we will not show mercy to these hostages.'"

The middle section of the verse describes the king instructing the Ninevites to change their ways. The king understands that simply fasting and sitting in ashes covered in sackcloth will not be sufficient to receive forgiveness from God. His approach follows the prophecies of Isaiah. Earlier in chapter 38, I quoted Isaiah's denunciation of fasting, sackcloth, and ashes as the means to God's forgiveness. In 58:5–8, Isaiah goes on to say that God wants repentant people to turn to righteous living. "Then when you call out, the Eternal will answer" (Isaiah 58:9).

Malbim explains that after the people have changed their ways they must provide compensation to the harmed party. "For from the robbery the confession and the contrition have no effect until the robber returns what he has to its owner." A part of changing is accepting responsibility for cleaning up the mess we created before we changed.

We have seen the sailors change from the worship of their many gods to the worship of the One God of Israel. And now here we see the Ninevites change. Their change is not a small adjustment in their lifestyle; they turn away from a life of violence and choose a new direction. Responding to Jonah's warning, they recognize the evil of their ways. They express contrition. According to Malbim, they make restitution for the damages they have done.

Many of us have had the experience of a friend or a relative pledging to make a major change in their lives. We have heard the words "I will be different from now on. You will see I am not going to be that person you have known. I am starting on a new path. I promise." Way too often these bold, confident pledges lead to disappointment as our friends or relatives quickly resume their old familiar patterns of behavior. In our story the Ninevites actually do change. What gives them the ability to make such a major shift?

The text tells us, "They cried out to God with might." Unlike Rashi, Kimchi understands "with might" to mean "with all their hearts." Serving God with all our hearts does not strike us as unusual, especially to people who participate in Jewish worship services. When we recite *v'ahavta* (Deuteronomy 6:5), we remind ourselves to "love the Eternal your God with all your heart and with all your soul and with all your might."

In the midrash to this Deuteronomy verse, the rabbis seek to understand what it means to love God with "all your heart" (Sifre 32). The biblical text simply could have said that we should love God with our hearts. The rabbis believe that the Torah does not contain any superfluous words. So adding *all* must add meaning. One of the sages suggests that "loving God with all our hearts" means that we should love God with our good inclination and with our evil inclination.

According to the rabbis of the Talmud, God created human beings with two opposing inclinations—one pushing us to do good and the other pushing us to do evil. The rabbis point to the word used in Genesis 2:7 to describe the creation of the original human being. The word *vayyeitzer* is written with two *yuds* in the middle of the word, where one *yud* would be sufficient. The rabbis believe that just as the Torah does not contain any extra words, it also does not contain any extra letters. The rabbis explain that one *yud* represents *yetzer hatov*, the good inclination, and the other *yud* represents *yetzer harah*, the evil inclination (TB Berachot 61a).

In the midrash sages explain that *yetzer harah* is a necessary part of the human personality. It includes our passions and desires, which move us to action. The midrash includes a fanciful story in which the residents of a town succeed in locking up the *yetzer harah* in order to improve the quality of life. To their surprise, while the *yetzer harah* was locked up, no women became pregnant, no one built a house, and no one went to work (Genesis Rabba 9:7).

The challenge for us is not to try to eliminate our *yetzer harah* but rather to keep it under control and to use its energy for positive ends. We need to use both our *yetzer hatov* and our *yetzer harah* to make changes in our lives.

Decades ago as a camp counselor, I learned a helpful strategy for responding to a camper who was acting out. I learned how to take his *yetzer harah*'s negative energy—disrupting activities to call attention to himself—and turn it into positive energy. If I had tried to use my strength of will to combat his strength of will, we would have gotten nowhere. We would have only created a loud and difficult situation. Rather than standing before him as a barrier, I stepped aside so that his energy carried him past me. If he needed to be the center of attention, I could put him in charge of the next activity. That way his *yetzer harah* could be put to use for his own benefit and for the benefit of the entire group.

According to the familiar saying, if we always do what we have always done, we will always get what we always got. We have the power to change, to reshape our lives. Jonah changed. The Ninevites changed. We can change.

41

The Fred Bob Principle

What Circumstances Will Lead to Success?

"Who knows but that God may turn and relent? He may turn
back from His wrath, so we do not perish." —JONAH 3:9

In the original Hebrew it is not clear to whom the opening phrase
of our verse "Who knows" (*Mi yodaiah*) refers. It could be read as
a rhetorical question, "Who knows?" Some of the commentators
take a different approach. They read it as a declarative phrase, "He
who knows."

Rashi understands the subject of the sentence to be not God but
rather those Ninevites who are sinners. "The one who has sins in
his hand shall repent."

Kimchi offers two ways to read the phrase. The first is that the
Ninevites are speculating about God's response to their repentance:
"[Who knows] perhaps God will have mercy on us in response to our
repentance from our evil deeds." The second possibility is that it refers
to former sinners among the Ninevites: "Or it could be explained,
the ones who know the paths of repentance will repent and the God
of Blessing will have mercy." Kimchi supports this interpretation by
quoting from the Targum: "And Targum Yonaton renders the verse
'Who knows there is here evidence of repentance of the Ninevites
settled correctly and mercy comes upon them from the Eternal.'"

Abarbanel also presents two ways of understanding this phrase:

This means to say "who knows which specific act of exploitation
and robbery was done by the hand of which specific Ninevite that
he will repent of it." Or it could mean who knows which of the
paths of repentance one should follow to repent before Hashem.

So that He will be merciful to them. For in this way Hashem will turn from His anger and they will not be lost. And from this the people of Nineveh feared God and understood the Divine decree in terms of its use of the word *overturn*. For the king had commanded that the people of Nineveh would overturn their deeds. So he says to them, perform his spiritual overturning and Hashem will overturn His decree. And the [intended] overturning of the city will not be carried out.

The standard translation makes the most sense to me. "Who knows but that God may turn and relent? He may turn back from His wrath, so we do not perish" (Jonah 3:9). The king does not promise the Ninevites that these acts of repentance will save them. He does not begin this sentence "I know." Rather, he humbly tells his people that this might work.

When we pull into a large, busy parking lot, sometimes my wife, Tammie, reminds me of the Fred Bob Parking Principle. My father believed that someone had to park right in front close to the door and it might as well be him. So before settling for a parking space in one of the back rows of the huge lot, we should first drive up to the front to see if we can find an open spot there.

A more generalized expression of the principle would be: If there is only one set of circumstances that will lead to success, we should act as if reality matches our hopes. This principle applies to a wide variety of human activities, from the most serious to the most light-hearted, from military planning to golf.

At the Civil War Battle of Chancellorsville, Gen. Robert E. Lee's Confederate forces were outnumbered by Gen. Joe Hooker's Union forces, two to one. Nevertheless Lee divided his forces, contrary to accepted concepts of military wisdom. Conventional military wisdom teaches that one should never divide one's forces in the face of the enemy; quite the opposite, a commander should concentrate his forces when going to battle. Following this principle becomes even more important when the enemy force is larger than your own.

But at Chancellorsville, Lee divided his force. He kept the main body of his troops in the line facing the Union troops so that Hooker would not notice anything unusual taking place. He then sent those troops under the command of Stonewall Jackson on a wide sweeping maneuver around the right wing of the Union army. When Jackson's troops emerged from the woods at the rear of the Union forces, they took them completely by surprise. The Yanks panicked and fled. Lee understood that he could only defeat the larger Union force through this unorthodox bold move, so that was the course he followed. He realized that sitting in place and waiting to be attacked would have led to his own destruction at the hands of the larger Union force. Lee had to act. He could not remain passive.

On the golf course the same principle applies. One of my golf buddies quotes a "Talmudic sage" we call "Rabeinu Nissan," who teaches that 100 percent of the putts left short do not go in. You have to hit the ball hard enough to reach the hole. Being too timid guarantees failure.

By their deeds the people of Nineveh prevented their destruction. The people and the king, the general population and the official leadership joined together to imagine the possibility of being saved. They did not know for a certainty that God would forgive them if they repented. Jonah had not structured his prophecy as a conditional if/then statement. He did not say, "If you do not repent in the next forty days, Nineveh will be destroyed." They imagined that the only path that could lead to their survival was to repent. By their actions they prevented the destruction of their world.

We can see more recent dramatic moments when human beings prevented the destruction of the world. In October 1962 President John Kennedy prevented nuclear war during the Cuban Missile Crisis when American U-2 spy planes had discovered that the Soviet government was in the process of installing missiles with nuclear warheads in Cuba just ninety miles from American shores. The Joint Chiefs of Staff advised Kennedy to bomb the missile sites in Cuba. But Kennedy believed that bombing the missile sites would lead to an all-out war with the Soviet Union. So instead of attacking the Soviet forces in Cuba, he ordered a naval blockade around the island nation to prevent further delivery of military supplies, and he demanded that the Soviets withdraw their nuclear missiles from Cuba.

During the crisis the American administration received two key letters from Soviet leader Nikita Khrushchev. One letter sent through secret channels suggested the possibility of negotiations. The other letter, broadcast publicly, was belligerent. The president's advisors tried to distill Khrushchev's actual intentions from the conflicting messages. Kennedy chose to believe that the pro-negotiation letter expressed Khrushchev's real position. In that letter Khrushchev wrote:

> Mr. President, we and you ought not now to pull on the ends of the rope in which you have tied the knot of war, because the more the two of us pull, the tighter that knot will be tied. And a moment may come when that knot will be tied so tight that even he who tied it will not have the strength to untie it, and then it will be necessary to cut that knot, and what that would mean is not for me to explain to you, because you yourself understand perfectly of what terrible forces our countries dispose. Consequently, if there is no intention to tighten that knot and thereby to doom the world to the catastrophe of thermonuclear war, then let us not only relax the forces pulling on the ends of the rope, let us take measures to untie that knot. We are ready for this.

President Kennedy chose to believe that this personal letter expressed Khrushchev's real position. He understood that only one set of circumstances could avoid World War III, so he chose to act as if reality matched his hopes. And he succeeded.

In our own lives we do not have to bear the burden of leading the free world or even the city of Nineveh. We do not command armies in battle. But we face the challenges of our own real-life problems. Sometimes these problems seem to be overwhelming. We need to look for possible solutions, even unlikely solutions. If we see only one set of circumstances that will lead to success, we should act as if the actual facts match those circumstances.

In response to Jonah's announcement of their imminent destruction, the leaders and the people of Nineveh searched for a possible means to save themselves. They understood that their only hope depended on believing that God would forgive them if they repented. We should not let what seem like overwhelming challenges to paralyze us. We should not sit still and wait for what we fear will be our inevitable defeat. We should seek out a path that will save us and move forward.

42

Bringing Water to Our Lives

Do We Appreciate Those Who Help Us?

God saw what they did, how they were turning back from their
evil ways. And God renounced the punishment He had planned
to bring upon them and did not carry it out. —JONAH 3:10

The text uses the same Hebrew word, *vayinachem*, to describe God's
change of heart and the Ninevites' change of heart. In connection
with the Ninevites' shift, we understand the term to mean "repented."
This is the standard use of the term. But would it be appropriate to
speak of God repenting? Rashi suggests a slightly different reading
of the word: God changes intention concerning the evil that had
been announced for Nineveh and turns from it.

The text says that God saw their repentance. What specifically did
God see? For one cannot see repentance; one cannot see a change of
heart. Ibn Ezra explains that "[God saw] that they believed in him.
And so it is in [the weekly Torah portion] Yitro, [where the text says
'before God']" (Exodus 18:12). In this section of the book of Exodus,
Jethro, the father in-law of Moses, a non-Israelite, comes to meet
Moses in the wilderness after the Exodus. He hears from Moses of
God's acts of redemption. Jethro praises God's redemptive power
and offers a sacrifice. Ibn Ezra argues that the devotion of the Ninevites here is similar to the devotion of Jethro there. What did God
see? He saw the Ninevites offering sacrifices to the One God as
Jethro had done.

Kimchi responds to this question of what God saw in a different
manner. According to Kimchi, "[God saw that the Ninevites turned
away] from their evil path in general, [and] from all the evil and violence they made a complete repentance." As our sages said, "He who

steals a beam and builds upon it a great building undermines the entire building when he returns the beam to its owner" (Tosephta Baba Kamma 10:5).

Abarbanel understands the repentance of the Ninevites as being more limited. He does not imagine the Ninevites bringing sacrifices to the One God of Israel:

> Their king does not worship Hashem, the Honored. And they do not remove idols and images of gods from their land. For they continually remain strong in their false faith. "And God saw their deeds." This means to say that in the commandments concerning relations between them and their neighbors, they repented from their evil ways. But they did not repent in their faith. And despite all of this, God relented from all the evil that was to be done [to the Ninevites] for was not the decree [of destruction] concerning the violence of their hands?

One might have expected that the full repentance of the Ninevites described in this chapter would also include them renouncing the worship of idols and the acceptance of the one true God. But the chapter contains no such mention. In an earlier century, Ibn Ezra also noticed this silence of the text but interpreted it in a much different way, concluding that the Ninevites had been worshippers of the one true God all along.

Rashi, Kimchi, and Ibn Ezra view the Ninevites as fully turning toward the One God of Israel, while Abarbanel sees the Ninevites' turning as less than fully complete. Abarbanel's less positive view of the Ninevites might have been affected by a distressing event in his life: Don Isaac Abarbanel was a leader of the Jewish community of Spain in the late fifteenth century. He advised Ferdinand and Isabella, and their decision to expel the Jews from Spain shocked him. They ignored all that he had done for them and all that the Jews had done for Spain. This life experience may be the source of his less positive assessment of the repentance of the Ninevites.

Sometimes people do not realize how much they have benefited from another's efforts until that person disappears from the scene. Our tradition provides a clear example of this dynamic. In Numbers 20:1 we read, "Miriam died there and was buried there." And then in the next verse we read that "the community was without water." The sequence of events drew the attention of our sages. The Torah itself does not connect these two events, but they did. Rashi assumes that there must be a link between the death of Miriam and the immediate lack of water. "From this we learn that all forty years, they had a well because of the merit of Miriam." The midrash presents Miriam's well as an expression of God's appreciation for Miriam's devotion.

The rabbis say that Miriam prophesied that Moses would be born. When the baby Moses floated down the Nile in a basket, Miriam stood guard. After the Israelites crossed the divided sea, Miriam led the people in a song of rejoicing. She earned great merit. During the forty years the Israelites spent in the wilderness, they needed water. The Torah text does not explain how they found water wherever they went. The midrash (Mekhilta de-Rabbi Ishmael, Beshalah 5) provides the answer. As a reward for all that she had done, God provides Miriam with a well. Wells generally remain in one place, but Miriam's well was a Divine gift; it moved. Wherever the Israelites traveled in the wilderness, the well went with them, but when Miriam died, the well ceased to exist. Without Miriam, there was no more water. God had provided the well because of all that Miriam had done, not because the Israelites deserved it. The waters of Miriam's well kept the people alive. But they did not associate the water with Miriam's merit. They took the unlimited supply of water for granted. The disappearance of water following Miriam's death stunned them. They did not understand what had happened.

In our own lives we may take for granted blessings we receive because of the merits of others. People die and leave our lives. But people also leave our lives in other ways and for other reasons. A coworker changes jobs or a friend moves away. When people leave, we often miss them in unexpected ways. Perhaps we did not appreciate what they had done for us when they were with us. We did not recognize the ways they sustained us until they stopped doing so.

The Bible includes stories of the general community not appreciating what a Jewish person had done for them. In Exodus 1:8 we read that a "new king arose over Egypt who did not know Joseph." The rabbis discuss the full meaning of the phrase. In Midrash Rabba a sage says the text does not simply mean that this new Pharaoh had never met Joseph, but rather that he pretended to know nothing of Joseph and the benefits that Egypt had received as a result of Joseph's management during the years of famine. He did not want to demonstrate any goodwill to the Israelites of his own time.

In the Purim story we read about Mordecai turning in the conspirators, Bigthan and Teresh, who were plotting to kill King Ahasuerus. Mordecai's action saved the king's life. However, this contribution does not save Mordecai from Haman's plan to kill all the Jews of the Persian Empire. The king does reward Mordecai with a ride on a royal horse, but he does not show Mordecai the appreciation a ruler should show a person who saved his life.

We can see a similar dynamic is operating in modern Jewish history. Over the centuries Jews contributed in many ways to the culture and economy of many European countries. But their contributions meant nothing when the Nazis invaded and occupied these countries. Important local leaders there did nothing to try to save the Jews from Hitler's horrors.

In the book of Numbers we read of the lack of water for our people in the wilderness following the death of Miriam. The people were stunned; they did not realize how much they needed Miriam until she was gone. They never honored or thanked Miriam. But in our story God does pay attention to deeds of the Ninevites and rewards them. Let us in our lives be aware of those who nourish us while they are still with us. Let us appreciate those who bring water to our lives.

43

Seeing Evil

Can We Recognize Our Own Flaws?

This displeased Jonah greatly, and he was grieved. —JONAH 4:1

This verse contains a verb and a modifier from the same root. This would be an unusual sentence construction in English but quite typical in biblical Hebrew. A literal translation of the phrase would be "It was evil to Jonah a great evil." All published English translations convey the meaning of the Hebrew but lose the rhythm of the original. It is rendered "This displeased Jonah greatly" (NJPS), "But it displeased Jonah exceedingly" (RSV), or "But to Jonah this seemed very wrong" (NIV).

The verb *vayeira* and the adjective *ra'ah* come from the same three-letter root, *raish, eiyen, hey*, referring to evil. Often the Hebrew Bible uses this device of a root appearing in two forms in the same phrase. We understand this device to convey intense feeling or action. We can understand the repetition of this root to express the depths of Jonah's disappointment that God did not destroy Nineveh.

Kimchi provides other biblical examples of the use of this root in the same sentence. "This is similar to [another biblical verse which is read literally as] 'What he did was evil in the eyes of the Eternal' [but is understood to mean], 'What he did was displeasing to the Eternal' (Genesis 38:10). And [another example read literally is] 'Will cause evil to the eye of his brother' [but understood to mean] 'Shall be too mean to his brother' (Deuteronomy 28:54)." We can understand our phrase to mean, as in the NJPS translation, "Jonah was deeply displeased."

Nehemiah 2:10 uses a phrase similar to our verse to describe the reaction of local Persian officials to the arrival of Nehemiah in the

Land of Israel. "*Vayeira lahem ra'ah gedola, asher ba'adam lvakeish tova livnei Yisrael.* It displeased them greatly that someone had come with the intent of improving the condition of the Israelites." The text of Jonah replaces "*lahem,* to them" with "*Yonah,* Jonah."

Why is Jonah not filled with joy at the repentance of the Ninevites? Is he an anti-Ninevite? A straightforward reading of this verse would understand Jonah to be expressing self-centered wounded pride. He had declared the coming destruction of Nineveh, but God forgave the Ninevites. This approach is consistent with the selfish personal traits expressed by Jonah in chapter 1. But rabbis seek a positive motivation for this apparently negative response of Jonah.

For Rashi the "evil" is Jonah's fear that the Ninevites will misunderstand the situation. Rather than recognizing that their own repentance moved God to cancel the decree of destruction, they will conclude that Jonah does not in fact speak for God. "Jonah says, 'Now [that Nineveh has not been destroyed], the idolaters [the Ninevites] will say that I am a false prophet.'" Rashi resists those who would understand this verse to be an expression of Jonah's disappointment and damaged pride that God's mercy had caused Nineveh to be saved.

Other commentators take this to refer to Jonah's disappointment at what they understand to be the Ninevites' partial repentance. Ababanel explains:

And this is because Jonah thought that God would not repent of the decree upon them [to destroy Nineveh] unless they repented of their evil ways in faith [idol worship] and in deeds [violence]. But he saw that they remained strong in their idol worship and that they had not repented in terms of their relationship to God but only in terms of their relationship to each other. And despite this Hashem was merciful concerning the evil that existed in His thoughts. And are these categories equal? For idol worship is a more serious sin than the sins between them. And they did not repent from idol worship. So if this is the case, why does Hashem repent from the evil that was prophesied to be done to them? There is no other explanation except that He removes their sin and misdeeds and protects them in the pupil of his eye so that they will be the "rod of anger" and "staff of fury" (Isaiah 10:5) and He will use them to cleanse Israel. And the prophet complains in his heart to Hashem. Why is it His intention to destroy Israel for their practice of idol worship, but to the people of Nineveh He passes over their similar sin? And this is why it says, "It was evil to Jonah, a great evil, and it grieved him." It means to say that he saw in his eyes the great evil that was prepared to come upon Israel. And in the anger of the Holy One of Praise at human beings, He forgives and pities the Ninevites but maintains His wrath on Israel.

Abarbanel sees Jonah's disappointment stemming from his knowledge of the role that the Ninevites will play in the future destruction of the Northern Kingdom of Israel.

The rabbis make excuses for Jonah's behavior. They seek positive explanations for his apparently negative behavior. We make excuses for the behavior of those we admire. Presidents and prime ministers, mayors and legislators get away with lies, oversights, mistakes, and at times crimes, because people who support them will not hold them to account for their errors. We hear excuses for the lapses of our leaders. These excuses include "It is just the way she is." Or "I know that he really loves us. He does such good work." Our concern for their welfare or reputation motivates us to speak up in their defense just as the commentators speak up in Jonah's defense.

The Dwight Eisenhower Presidential Museum in Abilene, Kansas, tells the story of the thirty-fourth president's life. It begins with his childhood in Abilene and through words and artifacts shows the path that led him to become the Supreme Commander of the Allied troops in Europe during World War II. The museum emphasizes Eisenhower's years as president, telling of his many accomplishments: beginning the interstate highway system, providing steady leadership during the Cold War, and overseeing the economic expansion of the 1950s.

But it devotes only one small corner of one gallery to the shortcomings of the Eisenhower administration. One wall presents Eisenhower's mixed response to school desegregation and highlights the positive by telling of his use of federal troops to enforce the court order to desegregate schools in Little Rock, Arkansas, in September 1957. The display does not dwell on Eisenhower's personal "go slow" reaction to the application of the Supreme Court's *Brown vs. Board of Education* decision.

Another wall explains that while Eisenhower privately expressed his "disgust" at Senator Joe McCarthy's witch hunts, he did not publicly denounce him, in order to maintain the unity of the Republican Party. During the 1952 presidential campaign, Eisenhower spoke in Appleton, Wisconsin, Joe McCarthy's hometown. Senator McCarthy had recently attacked former secretary of state George C. Marshall, calling him "a man steeped in falsehood." General Marshall had been Eisenhower's friend and mentor throughout his military career. The original draft of Eisenhower's speech for that day contained a defense of Marshall and a criticism of McCarthy, but Eisenhower skipped the portion of the speech about McCarthy to avoid offending his supporters. Historians report that Eisenhower always regretted that decision. The museum does not mention this aspect of Eisenhower's reaction to McCarthy because it would depict Eisenhower as choosing political expediency over moral principle and loyalty to a friend.

When we make excuses for the negative actions of those we admire, we allow them to duck responsibility for their actions. We may feel that we are being generous to them, but in truth by portraying them as flawless, we create unrealistic expectations of them and unrealistic expectations for ourselves. In truth all people have flaws including Jonah, Dwight Eisenhower, you, and me. Rather than making excuses or issuing denials, we should acknowledge our flaws and our mistakes.

For Jews, Yom Kippur provides an annual opportunity for us to atone for our sins. The holy day appears on every Jewish calendar for every year in ink. We do not write Yom Kippur tentatively in pencil just in case we do not commit sins that year. We know that we have flaws, and we will continue to make mistakes.

44

Playing a Part

How Do We Shape the Narrative of Our Lives?

> He prayed to the Eternal, saying, "O Eternal! Isn't this just
> what I said when I was still in my own country? That is why
> I fled beforehand to Tarshish. For I know that You are a
> compassionate and gracious God, slow to anger, abounding
> in kindness, renouncing punishment." —JONAH 4:2

Too often when we enter into a conversation, we are not certain if the other person is telling us the truth. Are they making up a story for effect, or are they relating an actual event from their life? Are they sharing their actual honest opinion with us, or are they making something up to get a desired reaction from us? In this verse Jonah seems to be speaking "creatively" to God.

Throughout the Hebrew Bible this verse's first word, "He prayed, *Vayitpaleil*," introduces a petition to God for protection and salvation. In 4:2 the text uses this word to introduce Jonah's petition to God for renewed life. (Ironically, in the continuation of this prayer in 4:3, Jonah petitions God for death.) Here Jonah is saying, "Isn't this just what I said when I was still in my own country?" referring to his knowing that God would forgive the Ninevites. Chapter 1 does not include any record of Jonah actually saying this. One might see this claim of Jonah, that he foresaw the course of events, as extremely self-serving. But the commentators again rise to Jonah's defense. Rashi sees Jonah as thinking, "I knew that if they returned to You in repentance, You would not destroy them, and I would become a liar in their eyes."

In his explanation of this verse, Abarbanel again ties Jonah's mission to Nineveh, the Assyrian capital, to the coming destruction of the Northern Kingdom of Israel at the hands of the Assyrian Empire. Abarbanel imagines Jonah saying:

> It is that all this slowness to anger and goodness that You have done for Nineveh is not out of Your love for them and is not because of justice of their pleas. But rather it is entirely "on my land." As it says, You are abundant in mercy to the Assyrians so that you will bring them "on my land," the land of Israel to destroy it. Thus I hastened to flee towards Tarshish. For I knew that because of my land You would be to Nineveh, "Gracious and compassionate slow to anger abounding in mercy." You will relent on the evil [that I declared would occur in forty days].

Malbim takes the opportunity again to raise the limited nature of the Ninevites' repentance. He points out that the text does not mention the Ninevites giving up the worship of idols. Malbim imagines Jonah saying to God:

> You forgave them immediately at the time of the decree from the side of mercy and patience even though they would not perform repentance in a proper way. Behold they did not perform repentance for the sin of idolatry; nevertheless, You did not bring upon them the evil of destruction because you had already forgiven them their evil; thus for a small improvement in their behavior you cancelled the decree. I did not flee because I thought that they would perform a proper repentance. In that case I would not have refused to go on a mission to turn sinners from their path. [I refused to go] only because I knew that they would remain worshippers of idols and you would not destroy them. For that reason I did not want to go on the mission.

Jonah's description of God's forgiving nature in the concluding phrase of this verse comes from Exodus 34:6. The Exodus passage continues to praise God's kindness but also says that God does "not remit all punishment but visits the iniquity of the parents upon the children." Our author chooses not to include that contrasting image.

Instead he maintains the message and concludes the verse describing God as "renouncing punishment." In Jonah 3:10 these words from "and God renouncing punishment" describe God forgiving Jonah. Here in 4:2 our author uses these same words, ironically, to describe Jonah's disappointment that God has forgiven the Ninevites.

Jonah claims that he predicted God's Divine forgiveness at the beginning of the story. But the text of chapter 1 does not record Jonah saying any such thing. As a matter of fact, in chapter 1 Jonah does not say anything at all when God calls him; he just runs away. Jonah has a creative memory. Jonah, with colossal *chutzpah*, says to God, "I knew this was going to happen." How could he have known that the Ninevites would repent? The repentance of the Ninevites is an unprecedented act. This is a self-justifying declaration attempting to turn his fearful flight into an act motivated by a clear vision of the future.

Sometimes we remember the past to our advantage. We retell stories in such a way that we become the hero. And sometimes when we hear someone else shift a story, we may think, "Wait a minute! That is not how it really happened. You were not the one who knew how to kindle a fire with just a couple of sticks! That was not you; it was our Charley!"

I have a friend, Billy, who does this so often that I think of a visit to Billy as "Adventures in Billyland." When I enter Billy's home I have to leave any expectation of historic truth at the door. When Billy tells a story, it is inevitable that Billy will become the hero. He will figure out the problem that no one else could figure out, or he will have a connection to just the important person who can intervene in the dire situation being described. I learned years ago that the connection between his descriptions of an event and what actually took place are very thin at best.

Woody Allen created a character named Zelig who takes the Billy approach to a whole other level. In Allen's film *Zelig*, the main character is, in film critic Vincent Canby's words, "a man so completely and so pathologically without any identity of his own that, without conscious effort, he takes on the physical, mental, and emotional characteristics of any strong personality he's with." Emmanuel Levy explains, "He is first observed at a party by F. Scott Fitzgerald, who notes that Zelig related to the affluent guests in a refined accent and shared their Republican sympathies, but while in the kitchen with the servants he adopted a ruder tone and seemed to be more of a Democrat. He soon gains international fame as a 'human chameleon.'"

We should see Billy and Zelig as cautionary tales of people who lose their own genuine identity in twisting reality. We do not have to shift our identity and twist stories to present ourselves in creative ways. We should develop confidence in our actual selves.

Life is not playing a role. According to a Hebrew Union College urban myth, a grizzled old professor prepares young rabbinic students for their first pulpits. He tells them, "Just be yourself. Unless you are a shmuck—then be someone else." In truth we need to find a positive way to be ourselves. We need to grow in self-awareness, understanding our strengths, and then ride those waves. This means that on occasion we need to change to meet new circumstances. We cannot simply insist that circumstances are the way we want them to be.

Unexpected circumstances have provided me with opportunities to grow. Many years ago our family drove to northern Michigan for a summer vacation. One afternoon I had the brilliant idea to take the children to pick cherries. I knew that they would enjoy picking and eating sweet Bing cherries. After a long drive we reached the orchard and discovered that we would in truth be picking sour cherries. Since I was not prepared to explain to my young children that we would not be picking cherries after all, we went ahead and filled a few buckets to overflowing with sour cherries.

When we arrived back at our cabin, the children proudly showed their mother all the cherries we had picked. After the children went out to play. I asked my wife what we should do with them. She told me that they would be perfect for cherry pies. Since I had been so gung ho for this outing, I understood that this baking would be my project as well. That afternoon I learned how to bake a cherry pie. Over the years I have developed pie-baking skills. Now when our congregation has a goods and services auction, I offer my famous pies. My willingness to grow and acquire new skills in response to unexpected circumstances has added a new line to my resume: Pie Boss.

Jonah's creative memory allowed him to falsely reconstruct the past to fit his needs in his conversation with God. We can avoid this dishonest approach. Rather than insisting that the facts are as we want them to be, we can adjust our views and actions in light of new knowledge and experiences.

45

Getting Lost

How Do We Regain Our Path?

Please, Eternal, take my life, for I would rather die than live. —JONAH 4:3

In our own lives sometimes we feel we are on the right path; other times we feel lost, literally and metaphorically. In this story Jonah seems quite lost. He seems to be giving up on life.

Verse 3 continues Jonah's prayer begun in verse 2. In the first part of the prayer Jonah describes God's power. Now Jonah expresses his wish, his petition for Divine intervention. Most often prayers of petition express a request for life, for healing, for a saving act from God. But here Jonah asks for death. On board the ship, Jonah was prepared to die to save the sailors; he told the sailors to throw him overboard so they might live and only he would die. That was a heroic act. Here Jonah's request for death seems like a selfish act. God's decision to forgive the Ninevites has apparently wounded Jonah's pride. He publicly predicted the destruction of Nineveh, and God disappointed him by forgiving the repentant sinners. Jonah cannot bear the shame; he cannot live in a world with forgiven Ninevites.

The commentators see a different motivation for Jonah's death wish. Ibn Ezra and Kimchi provide parallels from other biblical stories to show that Jonah's response is not unusual. Ibn Ezra explains, "Since he sees that Israel will not repent, he fears that evil will befall them. Therefore he prays, 'Take my soul' in the manner of 'be kind to me.' This is similar to what Elisha did in his anointing of Chaza'ail." Chaza'ail was a king of Aram whom God sent to attack the Israelites as a punishment for their misdeeds. Earlier God instructs Elijah to anoint Chaza'ail as king (1 Kings 19:15). Elijah does not complete this task during his remaining days on earth. Elisha carries on for him. When Elisha comes to anoint Chaza'ail as king, he cries, for he understands that this person will be God's agent to bring suffering on the Israelites (2 Kings 8:7f). So here in our text Jonah is upset because he realizes that God will now use the Ninevites to destroy the Northern Kingdom.

Kimchi takes a similar approach. "So I will not see the evil of Israel. This is similar to Moses our teacher, servant of the Eternal when, in response to the Israelites building the golden calf, he says to God, 'Now if You will forgive their sin, well and good. But if not, erase me from the record that you have written' (Exodus 32:32). And it is similar to Moses' response to the Israelites complaining about the manna: 'Kill me rather, I beg You, and let me see no more of my wretchedness'" (Numbers 11:15).

Abarbanel returns to his main theme of reading the Jonah story in the context of the coming destruction of the Northern Kingdom at the hands of the Assyrians. He imagines a longer soliloquy:

> Jonah says, "This means to say that now, after the question of rescue [of the Ninevites has been resolved], You will pour out Your wrath on my land. And the Assyrians will be your 'staff of fury'" (Isaiah 10:5). [Jonah says to God,] "Since I have already performed my mission now from my illness which sickens me. [And now take my soul from me for better is my death than my life. So that I will not see evil you will bring upon my people and the destruction of my homeland."] Now it is clarified that the evil that Jonah feels is not from the forgiving of Nineveh but rather from what he sees as the intention of the Holy One of Praise to do with Nineveh, to use it to destroy Israel. And because of this he requests death so that he will not see the destruction of [the ten] tribes of the Northern Kingdom by the hands of the Assyrians.

These two ways of reading Jonah's disappointment leave us with a Jonah feeling lost. Either he feels lost because of his wounded pride, or he feels lost because he has contributed to impending suffering of the Israelites. In the belly of the big fish, Jonah proclaimed his closeness to God and his sense of purpose. But now he feels lost.

In our own lives sometimes we feel we are on the right path and other times we feel lost, literally and metaphorically. I pride myself on my sense of direction. Only once have I been literally so lost that I needed to be rescued.

A few years ago an Israeli relative took my daughter Abby and me for a two-hour hike in the Golan Heights through Nahal El Al, a beautiful gorge in the mountains above the Kinneret (Sea of Galilee). The hiking trail generally follows a river that winds its way through the gorge. Our relative told us that we would see two waterfalls: a black waterfall that flows over black basalt rocks and a white waterfall that flows over white limestone rocks. We carefully followed the blue trail markers along the riverbed. We saw the black waterfall from above and then from below. We saw the wild flowers of the Golan. Then we hiked toward the white waterfall. We could hear it, but could not see it. We followed a branch of the trail that led away from the riverbed, higher up the south side of the valley to get a view of the falls.

We saw the white waterfall from above. It was truly a great view. But as we continued along the south side of the ridge, the trail seemed to be disappearing. Looking across the gorge to the other side, we saw what appeared to be the continuation of the trail. Why were we on the south side of the gorge if the continuation of the trail was on the north side of the gorge? We realized we had lost the trail. We tried to find it. We could see where we wanted to be, but it was not clear how to get there. We tried climbing down the side of the gorge to cross the river. This seemed promising, but we came to a cliff and had to turn back.

We tried to retrace our steps to find where we had turned off the trail. We tried climbing up the gorge. We came to a barbed wire fence.

We were quite lost, and the sun was setting. We were dressed and equipped for a brief daytime hike. It was getting dark and turning cold. We were getting hungry. We did not have jackets. We did not have flashlights. We did not have food. But we did have cell phones. Our relative called his wife to find help for us. She contacted Golan Rescue.

We sat above the white waterfall waiting for help. Time passed. We heard sounds of the night. We sat there shivering, trying to decide if we were listening to hyenas or jackals.

After a while in the distance we saw flashlights. They got a bit closer and stopped, still probably half a mile away. They did not see us. They were across the gorge. We could now see their flashlights clearly. We called to them, but the sound echoed off the sides of the gorge. They waved their lights back and forth but not in our direction.

I took out my cell phone, turned it on, and held it up in their direction. They saw the phone. They waved their flashlights in our direction. They called out that they were on their way. They told us not to move. It took another forty minutes for them to get to us. They had to climb down their side of the gorge, cross the river, and climb up our side of the gorge to reach our spot.

I expected that our rescuers would be young Israeli soldiers. But it was a man in his fifties and his two teenage children. They told us we were the second group they had rescued that day. They explained that we had lost the marked trail when we left the riverbed to climb up the gorge. In truth we were lost long before we realized we were lost. They gave us flashlights and led us out. We walked down our side of the gorge, back to the marked trail, across the river, and up the other side of the gorge. We completed our two-hour hike in five hours.

Jonah feels so lost that he gives up and asks God to take his life. Jonah does not ask God to help him. He does not seek a way out of the gorge. When we feel that lost, we should not give up. We should act to help those who want to help us. We should wave our lights, so that they can find us.

46

Narcissism

What Is Our Place in the World?

The Eternal replied, "Are you that deeply grieved?" —JONAH 4:4

The meaning of the word *heiteiv* in God's question is not obvious. The NJPS translation renders it "deeply." Ibn Ezra explains: "This is similar to 'I . . . broke it, *heiteiv,* grinding it thoroughly' (Deuteronomy 9:21). This grinding is full and complete." This verse from Deuteronomy describes the destruction of the Golden Calf. Ibn Ezra points out that in the Deuteronomy verse the word *heiteiv* is used to explain the full extent of the grinding process. Therefore we can see that here in our verse it is used to explain the full depth of Jonah's despair.

Kimchi provides another example of this use of *heiteiv.* "Thereupon all the people of the land went to the Temple of Baal, they tore down its altar, and its images they smashed to bits" (2 Kings 11:18). And there are those who connect *heiteiv* with *tov* [good]. They explain it to mean "Does the good I do to them grieve you?" And Targum Yonaton, drawing upon the context of its use in this verse, renders it like "*halachada.*"

Ibn Ezra asks, "And what is the reason God asks why you are upset about this?" Yafet ben Ali says [that God's question should be understood as meaning], "so it angers you that I am good to those to whom I want to be good?" This is vanity! God's question in this verse is not an inquiry by which God seeks information concerning Jonah's emotional state. But rather it is an expression of God's amazement at Jonah's self-centered attitude. "[God asks Jonah], 'Are you very grieved?' And He does not say any more than this. God could say that in a little while I will show you a sign that it is not according to the law that you should be grieved concerning my forgiveness to the repentant."

Abarbanel explains, "And here Hashem rebukes Jonah for his anger by saying, 'Are you deeply grieved?' It means to say that there is an evil aspect to your character that it deeply angers you that I am good to Nineveh. And that it angers you that I am good to whom I want to be good. That is not the way of a good person to be angered by the good [done by God], for 'The Eternal is good to all and His mercy is upon all His works'" (Psalms 145:9).

Jonah should not be surprised that God does good. God speaks sarcastically to Jonah: "Is it good for you to be so grieved?" Jonah's self-centered grief stuns God. Jonah has become the Hebrew Bible's version of Narcissus. In Greek mythology Narcissus falls in love with his own reflection in a pool of water. He loves the image so deeply he cannot leave the side of the pool. Narcissus has been immortalized in the term *narcissism*.

In Woody Allen's movie *Scoop*, a character who used to believe in Judaism but now has converted to another religion describes his shift in belief. Sid Waterman says, "I was born into the Hebrew persuasion, but when I got older I converted to narcissism."

I encounter many people who have maintained their Jewish identity but have also become followers of "narcissism." At times Jewish ritual moments become centered on the person rather than on the truly holy. I hear "horror stories" from colleagues about bar/bat mitzvah celebrations that turn into adulation of the child and a demonstration of wealth, rather than a celebration of the child being called to the Torah.

A popular literary example of a narcissistic life is known in Spanish as Don Juan and in Italian as Don Giovanni. He appears throughout the centuries in plays, stories, and operas. Mozart's opera *Don Giovanni* tells the story of this self-centered nobleman who seduces whomever he pleases, treating men and women as mere playthings. He cares only about his own pleasure and entertainment. He cares nothing about the impact of his actions on other people. In the opening scene of the opera he is attempting to seduce Donna Anna, the daughter of the Commendatore. Donna Anna cries for help, and the Commendatore comes to his daughter's aid. He fights a duel with Don Giovanni, who kills him. The Commendatore's death does not trouble Don Giovanni at all. He continues to seduce and scheme.

Later in the opera Don Giovanni taunts a statue of the Commendatore in the cemetery and afterwards he orders his servant to invite the statue to join him for dinner. That evening Don Giovanni hears a knock on his door. The statue of the Commendatore enters and offers Don Giovanni a last opportunity to repent of his narcissistic sins. Don Giovanni refuses. The Commendatore grabs hold of Don Giovanni and drags him down into hell. In opera, evildoers pay for their sins.

Narcissism has become so much a part of our way of life that its absence can seem stunning. A few years ago the national convention of the Reform Rabbis was held in San Diego. One of my colleagues who serves as an admiral in the Navy Reserve arranged for some of us to visit a few active-duty Navy ships. We went aboard a missile cruiser, a helicopter carrier, and a nuclear submarine. On each ship we met with officers and members of the crew. I went on the tour to see the ships, but I was most moved by the sailors. I did enjoy climbing around the ships, particularly the submarine. It was certainly cool to look through the periscope. But aboard our guide, the USS *Topeka*, the engineering officer, Lieutenant Kim, impressed me. He showed us around his submarine with great pride and enthusiasm. He explained that he was a recent engineering graduate of Stanford University and that he was proud that the Navy trusted him to be in charge of a nuclear reactor.

One of the members of our group asked Lieutenant Kim, given all the lucrative opportunities surely available to him as a graduate of Stanford University, what did his parents think about him using education to serve in the Navy? Lieutenant Kim explained that his father had come to the United States as an immigrant from Korea with nothing. He had built a life here for himself and his family. He expected that each of his children would give back to the country. Lieutenant Kim told us that he could not imagine a higher calling than serving his country and being part of the crew of the best submarine in the fleet. Lieutenant Kim's patriotism and his commitment to his crewmates impressed the members of our group. Rarely do we encounter a young person with such a perspective on life.

A key element of leading a quality life is understanding that you are part of something larger than yourself. Jonah has a difficult time with this concept, although at times he can manage to connect to a larger reality. At the end of chapter 1 he seems truly concerned about the welfare of the sailors on the ship. During his prayer from the belly of the big fish, he seems to understand himself in relationship with God. But here he falls back into his self-centered world.

Don Giovanni never sees himself as part of something larger than himself. We do not have to follow the self-centered path taken by Jonah and Don Giovanni. We can be part of something larger than ourselves. I see the teenagers in the congregation gain a sense of belonging and a feeling of purposefulness through participation on a sports team or in the cast or crew of a play. As an adult, I have felt this feeling of purposefulness by taking an active role in political campaigns. We can be part of a community by becoming active in a congregation or civic group or by providing help to a friend or relative in need. We each need to remember that we are not the center of the universe. Our lives become more meaningful when we understand our role in the larger story.

47

Connecting the Dots

How Can We Make Sense of Our Lives?

> Now Jonah had left the city and found a place east of the city.
> He made a booth there, and he sat under it in the shade until
> he should see what happened to the city. —JONAH 4:5

The NJPS translation above solves a problem that confronts people who read the book of Jonah in the original Hebrew, which begins "*Vayeitzei Yonah min-ha'ir*, Jonah went out of the city." The commentators ask why this verse begins with the word *vayeitzei*, "went out." Surely Jonah left Nineveh immediately after issuing his proclamation contained in 3:4.

Ibn Ezra explains that the text returns to the earlier moment in the story "to recall the words of Jonah that he proclaimed before the completion of the forty days." According to Ibn Ezra, the sequence of the verses in this chapter does not follow the sequence of events as they unfolded. The conversation between God and Jonah described in verses 4:1–4 took place after Jonah's departure from Nineveh described here in 4:5.

Ibn Ezra supplies examples of similar usages of this construction from other parts of the Bible, such as "And he came upon a certain place" (Genesis 28:11). This verse describes the arrival of Jacob at Bethel, the site of his famous dream, during his journey from Canaan to Paddan-aram. The problem is that earlier in the chapter, in Genesis 28:5, the text reads, "He went to Paddan-aram." This suggests he left Canaan and arrived in Paddan-aram. Then in verse 11 Jacob is not in Paddan-aram but rather back in the middle of his journey. "Also Joseph took the two of them" (Genesis 48:13). This verse is from the story of Jacob blessing Joseph's two sons, Menasseh and Ephraim.

This verse says, "Joseph took," even though in Genesis 48:1 the text already says that Joseph "took his two sons." In these two Genesis verses we have verbs recalling events that had already taken place. In a similar manner *vayeitzei* in our verse recalls Jonah's departure from Nineveh, which had already taken place. Ibn Ezra understands that the events described in 4:1–4 took place after Jonah's departure from Nineveh described in 4:5. Ibn Ezra understands 4:5 to mean "Jonah had left the city" sometime earlier. The NJPS translation follows Ibn Ezra's reading of the verse.

Kimchi reads the text differently. He reads 4:5 to mean "Jonah left the city." As a result he understands 4:1–4 to describe activity that took place immediately following Jonah's announcement that "in forty days Nineveh will be overthrown," meaning while he was still in the city. The first four verses in this chapter work because, according to Kimchi, "The God of Blessing told him in the spirit of prophecy that He would relent from what He had decreed concerning them because they had repented from their evil paths." Kimchi explains why Jonah remained in the area. "And he sat in a place that was east of the city. Until he would see if perhaps they would not maintain their repentance and God's verdict would again be in force."

Abarbanel also rejects Ibn Ezra's approach. He supports Kimchi's reading of the text. "It would be more correct to explain that immediately after the proclamation of the prophet the people of Nineveh were roused to repent." They did not wait for the forty days to elapse. "And Hashem informed Jonah that He had relented from the evil while Jonah was still in Nineveh." Abarbanel explains why Jonah left Nineveh:

"And Jonah departed from the city" so as not to fraternize with the evil Assyrians. And he sat from before the city, to the east of the city. "And he made for himself a hut" so that he would sit there until he saw what would become of the city, for he thought that even though the people of Nineveh had escaped from the general destruction since Hashem had relented from evil that had been stated to be done. Behold they had not been cleansed or released from a punishment that could be brought to all of them or some of them or to the houses of their gods because of their ongoing idolatry.

Abarbanel points to a similar biblical story to help us understand this section of the Jonah story.

For in the case of the golden calf, Moses prayed before he descended from the mountain. And it says there, "And the Eternal renounced the punishment He had planned to bring upon His people" (Exodus 32:14). And after this, "And then the Eternal sent a plague upon the people" (Exodus 32:35). And Moses, our teacher, peace be upon him, had to sit on the mountain for forty days for their forgiveness.

And thus was the case of Jonah that he knew from Hashem that He had relented from the general overturning. He sat in the hut to see what might happen to the city. Would "The Eternal send a plague upon the people" (Exodus 32:35)? Would God punish some of the people as God had done in the incident of the golden calf? Or what else might happen?

According to Abarbanel, Jonah waits to see what God will do to the people of Nineveh.

I do not agree with Abarbanel and Kimchi. I find Ibn Ezra's explanation much more convincing. The action described in this verse must have taken place right after Jonah made his declaration in 3:4 He waits to see what will happen to Nineveh. In Hebrew there is no separate past perfect form to describe action that has already been completed; verbs in the regular past tense form are used for this purpose. So we can understand this verse to begin, "Now Jonah had . . ." We saw a similar construction earlier in 1:5. There the text describes Jonah falling asleep and the sailors throwing the cargo into the sea in response to the storm. We should read the second half of that verse as Jonah had fallen asleep, as we read this verse, "Now Jonah had left." As does the NJPS translation.

As Ibn Ezra makes sense out of this possibly confusing story, we need to make sense out of our experiences. As human beings we cannot live lives of unrelated random events. We need to be able to sort and categorize our experiences. We need to structure our reality. We have a need to connect the dots of our lives so that they form a picture. We need to see our lives as being part of a continuing narrative.

Despite my thirty-five years as a congregational rabbi, I still encounter new experiences in my life in the synagogue. Unanticipated things still happen at a bar/bat mitzvah that have never happened before. But no matter what happens, I have a mental category in which to place the new event. I know right away how to respond because something similar has happened before. I recall what I did then and whether or not it was effective.

When I am asked to officiate at a funeral, I sit with the family and ask them to tell me stories. I may already know the deceased quite well, or I may have become the officiating rabbi as the result of my connection to one of the mourners. In either case I want to hear the stories. Even if I am not going to be delivering a eulogy at the service, I want to hear them. The process of telling stories about the deceased's life helps shift the attention of the mourners from the circumstances of the death to the life of their loved one. I say, "Tell me the story of her/his life." Or I ask, "How did you meet your wife/husband? How did you come to live in our community? What did your parents enjoy doing together?" These simple questions elicit stories that together form the narrative of the deceased's life.

Some of us can view our lives as hinging on one key moment or one key year. Others see their lives as a series of chapters leading from one to another. We can see an illustration of this dynamic in a baseball question. Everyone can agree that Sandy Koufax is the greatest Jewish pitcher of all time. But who is the second greatest Jewish pitcher of all time, Ken Holtzman or Steve Stone?

Ken Holtzman pitched for fifteen Major League seasons. He won more games than any other Jewish pitcher, 174. He was a two-time all-star. He pitched on three pennant-winning teams. In his best season, 1973, he went 21–13 for the Oakland A's. Steve Stone pitched in the majors for eleven seasons. He won 107 games. But in 1980, he was 25–7 for the Baltimore Orioles. He won the Cy Young Award. In that one year he was the best pitcher in baseball.

So who was the second greatest Jewish pitcher of all time? Holtzman had a more successful career, but Stone had a better single season. Some of us will see the story of our lives to be closer to the Ken Holtzman storyline. Others of us will be closer to the Steve Stone storyline.

When we, in the midst of living our lives, can join together our stories to form a narrative, we have a stronger sense of purpose and meaning. When the events of our lives seem to be a collection of disconnected chapters, we become confused and disheartened. We want to be able to see how the chapters in stories of our lives lead from one to another. We should be able to imagine the chapters yet to be written describing the events of the years to come.

48

The Kikayon

What Can We Learn from a Plant?

And the Eternal provided a ricinus plant, which grew up over
Jonah, to provide shade for his head and save him from discomfort.
Jonah was very happy about the plant. —JONAH 4:6

I have an unusual last name. I have been told by more than one
hotel clerk, "Your last name can't be Bob," as if I would not know
my own last name. Most people assume that Bob is a shortened version of our original European name. They imagine that a relative
of mine chose Bob to have a more American name than Bobinsky
or Bobarov. But in truth Bob was our family's name in Lithuania. It
could have come from the first letters of the two words *ben brit*, son
of the covenant. This phrase could have simply identified my ancestor as a Jew. My former senior rabbi suggested that it came from the
first letters of the two words *bihairah b'yameinu*, meaning "quickly in
our days," generally used to describe the coming of the messiah. (I
have no such pretentions!) A leading Chicago rabbi insists that the
most likely source of our family's name is the Lithuanian Yiddish
word for bean, *bub*. So I may come from a long line of bean dealers.
I realize that I will never know for sure the origin and meaning of
my last name. Similarly the identity of the plant mentioned in this
verse may remain a mystery.

The commentators try to sort out the identity of the plant and its
relationship to God and Jonah. This verb, *vayaman*, "provided or
designated," is the same word used at the beginning of chapter 2 in
connection with the big fish. Rashi explains that it should be understood as "words of invitation," that is, God summoned the plant. The
Hebrew word *vayaman* has the same root as *manah*. A *manah* is a

portion. Here we can take it to mean "provided." The same word appears in the next two sentences to describe God summoning the worm and the hot wind. God acts as a stage manager cueing the players, the fish, the plant, the worm, and the wind when it is their moment to enter the action onstage.

Kimchi adds, "He caused it to sprout according to the hour. For even though he built himself a booth for shade, perhaps the branches of the booth dried out. For he dwelled there until the completion of the forty days." According to Kimchi, Jonah built the booth on the day of his proclamation that Nineveh would be destroyed within forty days. And then dwelled in it, waiting to see what would happen. "And He made this sign for him to teach him about the Divine decree. For He has mercy on all His creatures."

Abarbanel follows Kimchi in seeing the timing of the growth of the *kikayon* plant as a key element of the miracle. "And then the Holy One of Blessing prepared the *kikayon* plant that it would sprout there according to the hour. And Jonah rejoiced greatly, for he already had a hut under which he sat. And the sun was shining through the roof of the hut and striking his head. And as the branches of the roof of his hut dried, he would no longer have shade in it."

I have intentionally used the Hebrew word to describe the plant. The only time this word appears in the Hebrew Bible is here in the book of Jonah, so there is no consensus as to the exact identity of the plant. Kimchi provides several possibilities for the plant's identity:

> It is a tall and beautiful plant. Its leaves provide shade. In the Mishnah we read "not with the oil of a *kik* plant." And in the Gemara it is asked, "What is this *kik*?" Resk Lakish says, "It is the *kikayon* of Jonah." Rabbah bar Bar Channah says, "I saw this *kikayon* of Jonah which is like a *tzuliva*" (Shabbat 21a). And my father, my teacher and my mentor, Rabbi Joseph Kimchi, explained that it grows between the ditches of water. At the entrances of stores it is grown to provide shade. And from its kernels oil is made. Rabeinu Shmuel ben Hafni says it is a plant that is called in Arabic *aleveroa*,

[which we know as aloe vera]. The explanation of *tzuliva* I found in the responsa of the *gaonim*. It is a tree without fruit that grows in our area in abundance. And it has kernels. And from them oil is made, and everyone who has a cold drinks of it. And its name in Arabic is *alk'rua*.

Ibn Ezra says, "The sages of Spain say that it is a gourd, or a *kara*. [It is unknown to which type of plant this word refers.] And there is no need to know what it is."

No one knows what kind of plant the *kikayon* is. This is similar to the location of Tarshish and the species of the big fish. None of these details are known, and none of them are important. Tarsish is some city outside the Land of Israel, the fish is some giant species big enough to swallow a person, and the plant must be leafy enough to provide significant shade. Knowing the precise type of plant would not add to our understanding of the events of the story.

Kimchi explains the suffering from which the *kikayon* protects Jonah. "From the heat of the sun that struck and dried up the branches of the booth that was his source of shade."

Rashi points out that "there are those who say that because he stood in the belly of the fish for a long time the skin of his flesh was tender and could not withstand the heat." This approach explains why Jonah required more protection from the sun than would most other people.

Abarbanel connects Jonah's suffering here in verse 6 with the evil he felt in verse 1. "For he was sick as I have explained in my comment to verse 1. And when the sun would come with all its strength, he might die as he had requested of Hashem, may He be blessed. Therefore, in order to save him from his evil, this means to say, the evil of his illness and the evil of his request to die, came the *kikayon* plant. And Jonah rejoiced in it. As is the way of those with fever deriving great joy from cold objects."

Malbim explains that Jonah needed the *kikayon* because of the shortcomings of the booth that Jonah had built.

For the shade of the booth did not protect him very much from the sun. As is written, "He sat under it in the shade" (Jonah 4:5). It should be clarified that there was not shade in the entire booth, for the walls of the booth were not covered except for the side where the sun shone. And in the heat he had to sit under the eastern wall. And in the middle of the day there was no shade at all. The *kikayon* provided shade from above on his head to protect him. For his head was vulnerable to be injured by the heat of the sun.

This verse concludes by describing Jonah's reaction to the *kikayon*. He felt "a great joy." Jonah is not simply happy about the plant. He is very happy. His great joy is another example of exaggeration that we have seen earlier in the biblical book. Also he does not thank God for the plant. Either he does not notice that the plant grew in a miraculous manner, or he thinks it is just coming to him.

In 4:2 Jonah quotes Exodus 34:6 to describe God as "slow to anger." Here God demonstrates great patience with Jonah. God does not simply dismiss Jonah's objection to the Divine acceptance of the Ninevites' repentance. God uses the *kikayon* plant to teach Jonah to be concerned with the world beyond himself. We will see God explain this lesson explicitly to Jonah in the final verse.

Jonah reminds me of the people I regularly encounter who think only of themselves. One of my friends enjoys kidding around with people he meets. With the last name of Bob, I have heard many "jokes" about my name or—perhaps more accurately—the same jokes many times.

The most repeated joke is, "Wouldn't it have been funny if your parents had named you Robert?" Hearing this joke certainly does not wound me, but it also does not entertain me as much as the teller of the joke might imagine. Once I was at a desk in a hotel checking in. The staff member started with Bob jokes: Do you have a son named Dylan or Marley? Another staff member, a strikingly tall woman, interrupted her friend. She said, "Enough, stop with the jokes about his name. It is like people making height jokes to me.

I know that I am six feet tall." A person who insists on telling these annoying jokes cares only about appearing to be clever. He ignores the impact they have on the other person.

Jonah acts as if the whole world exists for his benefit. He imagines that the purpose of the Ninevites is to be punished so that his prophecy will be realized. He imagines that the *kikayon* plant has no value on its own, but rather sees its entire purpose in terms of the impact it has on him. Jonah has no sense of perspective or context.

Our lives develop much more texture when we see ourselves as part of a large whole. We each should avoid seeing ourselves as solo performers, better to view ourselves as being part of a large orchestra. Let's imagine that we play the violin. Sometimes the whole orchestra plays. Sometimes it is just the violins and the violas. Sometimes the reeds play, and we sit silently. And every once in a while I have a solo part. I do not stand at the center of the world; I am a very small part of a much larger whole.

49

Time, Time, Time

How Do We View the Length of Our Lives?

> But the next day at dawn, God provided a worm, which
> attacked the plant so that it withered. —JONAH 4:7

I am proud to be part of the baby boom generation. We have occupied center stage in American culture for many decades. As we enter retirement we can reflect on our impact. Will the impact of our lives be lasting, or will we be like the *kikayon* plant that withers one day after it appeared?

The author of the book of Jonah uses the word *vay'man*, "provided or designated," four times. It is used by the text to describe God providing the big fish in 2:1, the *kikayon* plant in 4:6, here the worm, and in the next verse the wind. Kimchi explains that God "arranged for the worm to be at the location of the plant at this specific time."

Ibn Ezra tells us that the "next day" refers to the day after "the day of his joy in the *kikayon* plant." Ibn Ezra explains that only one day passed from the appearance of the plant described in 4:6 and its destruction in 4:7, as will become clear in God's remarks to Jonah in 4:10. Kimchi describes how the worm attacked the plant. "It means to say that [the worm] attacked the lower part of the plant. After it stopped receiving moisture from the earth, it was cut and withered." The worm did not consume the entire plant. It ate the key part of the plant, causing it to die. Kimchi continues, "It had been used for [a source of] shade. Behold for one day he had this joy and by dawn the next day it was broken and withered." The worm attacks the *kikayon* plant "the next day at dawn." In the old English proverb, the early bird catches the worm. Here in our verse, the early worm catches the *kikayon* plant. God does not wait to get to work.

The Bible describes many key people getting up early to do God's work. In the binding of Isaac story, Abraham gets up early in the morning to set out on the journey (Genesis 22:3). When God sends Moses to confront Pharaoh, the Divine instructions specify time of day. Now the Eternal said to Moses, "Early in the morning present yourself to Pharaoh" (Exodus 8:16). Moses rose early and went up to Mount Sinai, as the Eternal had commanded him, and he took two stone tablets in his hand (Exodus 34:4). Joshua begins the seven processions around Jericho in the morning. "Then on the seventh day they rose at daybreak" (Joshua 6:15).

Jewish tradition teaches that we should be *mukdam l'mitzvah*, eager to fulfill God's commandment as soon as possible. So, for example, in the traditional community a *brit milah* takes place in the morning. Delaying the ceremony until the afternoon suggests that you are less than excited about fulfilling God's commandment.

Many people do not lead *mukdam l'mitzvah* lives. Many people are not *mukdam*, early, on any task. Quite the opposite, many people procrastinate. Procrastination is a widespread affliction. I used to be a terrible procrastinator. My mother could offer enthusiastic testimony of how I put off school assignments until the very last minute. I have generally filed my tax return late in the evening on April 15. In the old days I most likely would have said to myself, I will complete this chapter on procrastination later.

Why do we put things off? Jason A. McGarvey of Penn State sees one cause of procrastination as an "intense fear and avoidance of evaluation of one's abilities by others." When we are confident of a positive outcome, we have no reason to put off the project. When we doubt that the outcome will be positive, we wait as long as possible to get to the project.

Some people, when they assemble an agenda for a meeting, will put the "small items" first to get them out of the way, after which the group will be able to devote its attention to the major problems. I suggest the opposite approach. Let's begin with the most challenging question. When we have the most energy and the most time, let's consider the most difficult issue.

As I have grown older, I have procrastinated less and less. I have become more confident in my own judgment. In 1964 when I heard Mick Jagger sing, "Time, time, time is on my side, yes it is," I was fourteen years old, and I agreed with Mick. I confidently believed that time was on my side. Now in my mid-sixties, I relate more strongly to the words of Rabbi Tarphon, who taught, "The day is short, the work is much, the workers are lazy, the reward is great, and the Master of the house is pressing" (Pirke Avot 2:15). Rabbi Tarphon teaches that we should realize that our lives are short and we have much to do. Too many people are lazy. The benefits for working hard are worthwhile, and God has high expectations of us.

I was born in 1950 at the height of the postwar baby boom. With a 1950 birthday, I knew from a young age that I would turn 50 in the year 2000. I felt that my life was in tune with the counting of the years. We baby boomers grew up during the civil rights movement, and we came of age during the Vietnam War. Some of us served in the war, and others strove hard to avoid serving and to end the war. We listened to groundbreaking music during our formative years, the Beatles and Bob Dylan. We took Dylan's "Times They Are a Changing" seriously. When we were young, we believed that our generation was special. We felt "designated," like the fish, the *kikayon*, the worm, and the wind in Jonah's story. We felt that we were here for a purpose. We were certain that we would change the world.

Each of us should feel that we are here for a purpose. My Christian minister friends speak of "being called to the ministry." In the Jewish community we do not use that language, but we should all feel that we are on a mission. We should feel that our day-to-day lives are each part of fulfilling that mission. The Psalmist teaches us: "The span of our life is seventy years, or given the strength, eighty years. . . . They pass by speedily" (Psalm 90:10–11). We do not receive an outline of our lives on the day we are born. We do not know how long we will live or what problems we will have to confront.

As Rabbi Tarphon teaches, "The day is short." All of us, like the *kikayon* plant, are here only briefly. While we do not know exactly how long our day on earth will last, we should embrace Rabbi's Tarphon's challenge to understand that we have much to do. We each have our own set of tasks. Some of these tasks we have chosen. Other tasks have been placed upon us by circumstances beyond our control. In either case we should be *mukdam l'mitzvah*, eager to fulfill what life asks of us.

50

Facing Challenges

How Do We Use Our Strengths to Overcome Our Weaknesses?

> And when the sun rose, God provided a sultry east wind; and the
> sun beat down on Jonah's head, and he became faint. He begged
> for death, saying, "I would rather die than live." —JONAH 4:8

In this verse Jonah describes his difficult situation in very dramatic language. Earlier, in 4:3, Jonah expresses his desire to die. Here he returns to this most negative prayer. He asks God to take his life. Jonah seems to lack the inner resources to accept the personal disappointment caused by God's forgiveness of the Ninevites. Before explaining the situation to Jonah, God intensifies Jonah's suffering.

English translations describe the wind as sultry, vehement, scorching, or blasting. This variation in translation tells us that the original Hebrew word, *charishit,* might be unclear. This is not an adjective regularly used to describe the wind. The commentators seek to clarify its meaning. The Targum understands this word to mean "quieting." Rashi explains, "Our sages taught that at the time when this wind blows it silences all other winds." The root of this word is *chet-raish-shin,* which can mean silent or deaf. Ibn Ezra refers to "Rabbi Merinos [Rabbi Yonah ibn Janach], who said that it was so strong that hearing its roar deafened the ears." We should not mistakenly conclude that the wind was silent. Quite the opposite, it was so strong it was deafening. Abarbanel also points to the volume of this exceptional wind. "As if to say from hearing its roaring until it deafens the ears." Kimchi points to the strength of the wind. "And the explanation of *charishit* is that it was so strong that when it blew it made people deaf."

People who have lived in the Middle East during the summer understand this word from experience. On certain summer days a hot wind stifles all activity. Contemporary Israelis call this wind by the Arabic word, *chamsin*. To further test Jonah, God not only removes the *kikayon* (ricinus) plant but literally turns up the heat. God places Jonah in great discomfort. Kimchi explains, "An eastern wind is itself hot so that the impact of the sun becomes the impact of the sun and the wind together."

Our text describes Jonah as *vayitalaf*. Ibn Ezra explains that this word can be understood in two ways: it can mean "faint," which is similar to *titalafna*, "shall faint" (Amos 8:13). And it can mean "wrapped," as in "And she covered her face with a veil, *vatitalaf*, wrapping herself up" (Genesis 38:14). He goes on to explain the connection between the two meanings of the word as used in our verse: "He [Jonah] grew faint wrapped in his clothes."

Abarbanel explains the impact of the elements on Jonah's body. "As if to say that it brought him to critical condition. Which is the lack of life-giving air entering to his heart and the other organs, like the dead. Jonah saw that he had been brought to the gates of death." Kimchi describes the condition of Jonah's soul. "His soul was exhausted and he became quite stricken to the extent that he could no longer stand on his own because of the heat. His spirit was close to departing. He was close to death."

I would say that Jonah thinks that he is close to death rather than actually being close to death. Jonah is the most overly dramatic character in the Hebrew Bible. He seems to have concluded that without the *kikayon* plant his life has no meaning.

People respond to disappointments and tragedy in vastly different ways. Some, when they encounter a big obstacle or problem, seek a path that will allow them to continue walking forward, while others are thrown off course by the smallest bump in the road. I know a woman who lost two babies to cystic fibrosis, and her wonderful first husband died of cancer. She married another wonderful man, and a few years later he also died of cancer. She married a third wonderful husband and built a new life. She does not complain. She has always been a social leader in our community who tells entertaining stories and is a source of strength to others.

A few years ago I attended a retirement planning seminar for synagogue professionals. At one of the sessions the group leader asked the participants about our plans for our retirement years. I shared my pretty well thought through plan for how I would spend my time. I was also able to describe the steps I was taking at that time to lay the foundation for the plan. I had created opportunities for college teaching. I was completing a book that could lead to some guest scholar opportunities. And I had an interfaith solar energy project getting off the ground.

Another participant asked if she was doing something wrong because she did not have a retirement plan. I responded by saying that planning isn't for everyone, but it is for me. I always have a plan for just about everything I do. I plan vacations in great detail. I am not one to get to the destination and see which hotels have vacancies. Before we leave home, I have figured out a route; I know what we can see, what we can do and where we can stay. Often we diverge from the plan once the trip has started, but we always begin with a plan.

I understand that other people would find my approach restrictive. They would rather be spontaneous, making choices on the go. We need to honestly examine ourselves to see our strengths and weaknesses and then play to our strengths and try to avoid our weaknesses. This might sound obvious, but it can happen in subtle ways, too.

When I was in rabbinic school, students served congregations in small towns that were not large enough to support full-time rabbis. The students at the Hebrew Union College in Cincinnati served small congregations throughout the Midwest and the South, visiting them twice a month. Each spring the students held a draft to select their student pulpits for the coming year. In advance of the draft, the students currently serving each of these congregations would write a "scouting report" to help the next students choose the congregation that would be the best fit for them.

We each had our own concerns. Some of the students focused on transportation issues. Some of the congregations were "fly and drive." You had to first fly to Memphis and then drive to Jonesboro, Arkansas. Others like Marion, Ohio, were close enough to Cincinnati to be reached by car. Other students focused on accommodations. Some of the congregation put the students up in members' homes, while others arranged for hotel rooms.

My biggest concern was music. Many of the congregations expected the student rabbis to lead the singing during the services, and I have no skills whatsoever in that area. I could not allow myself to be put in that situation. So I chose Williamson, West Virginia, not because it was only a five-hour drive from Cincinnati, not because I was able to stay in the "historic" Mountaineer Hotel, and not because I wanted to spend my weekends in the home of the Hatfield-McCoy feud. I chose Williamson because the congregation had a music director who played the organ and led the singing.

If I had been forced to take a congregation where I would have needed to sing, my response would have echoed Jonah: "It is better for me to die than to live." We should try to understand our strengths and our weaknesses. We do not need to deny the existence of our weaknesses. I used my planning skills to carefully research the student pulpits to learn which ones expected their student rabbis to sing. Let us try to use our strengths to avoid being in situations that expose our weaknesses.

51

I Want to Be Big

Can We Learn Patience?

> And God said to Jonah: "Are you deeply grieved about the plant?"
> "Yes," he replied, "so deeply that I want to die." —JONAH 4:9

When we reflect back over our lives, we want to be able to see growth. A composer of some of the most popular worship melodies once told me that there is huge difference between the pieces he wrote at the beginning of his composing career and those he had written more recently. He began to write songs when he was still a teenager and did not know much about Jewish liturgy or musical composition. He was happy to tell me that he had grown over the years. Sadly Jonah does not seem to develop prophetic skills or understanding.

Here and in the following verse, the text uses this word from 4:1, *grieved*, to describe Jonah's sense of loss over the death of the plant. In this verse God asks the question sarcastically, "Are you deeply grieved?" Jonah seems oblivious to God's sarcasm. One might ask, why does God continue to speak with Jonah, who is so disappointing a prophet? In the book of Numbers, when Korach and his followers rebel against the leadership of Moses and Aaron, God punishes the rebels in a memorable manner. "And the earth opened its mouth and swallowed them up, and their households, and all Korach's people, and all their possessions" (Numbers 16:32).

God responds to Jonah differently. Ibn Ezra explains, "The Eternal continues to teach his prophet, even though he angers Him, because the Eternal is gracious."

Abarbanel examines Jonah's unusual prayer. "Jonah does not request life or health but rather death. And from another side, he is angry over the *kikayon* plant that 'is over and gone' (Song of Songs

2:11). For he had rejoiced in it. As a result Hashem rebukes him with His words in this verse." And these two things—his request for death and his anger at the destruction of the plant—seem to contradict each other. Abarbanel artfully attempts to untangle an apparent contradiction in Jonah's position:

> For God says, "Are you deeply grieved over the *kikayon* plant?" This means to say, if the situation is according to your words that death is good, why are you angry about the withering of the *kikayon* plant? And yet it appears that life is good in your eyes, since you rejoiced in the *kikayon* plant that lengthened your life and were angry by its removal that brought your death closer. And the prophet responded to Him, "I am greatly grieved to death." That is to say, I say to You, "Forever I am grieved unto death. And certainly I am grieved over the *kikayon* plant. Not on the issue of death but rather in terms of punishment and pain I would suffer until I die. And thus death is good, but the pain from the sun before death is what angers me."

So Jonah is not actually concerned about life and death in general. He is only concerned about his own personal comfort. As Jonah recited his prayer from the belly of the big fish, he seemed to be changing from being self-centered to appreciating his position in the context of the larger world. He certainly appeared to be deeply concerned about his relationship with God. But now as we approach the story's conclusion, Jonah appears to have reverted back to his earlier self-centeredness. Despite his experience in the belly of the fish, Jonah has not grown. And growth is an important key to a happy life.

The psychoanalyst Erik Erikson was best known for his theory of the stages of human psychosocial development. He explained that there is a basic conflict facing individuals at each of the eight stages in their personal development and that each stage contains important life events. According to Erikson, people suffer when they get stuck in any of these stages because they are not able to resolve the conflict or master the events. Since Erikson first presented his groundbreaking theories more than fifty years ago, many psychologists have offered their own theories about personal development. There is a wide range of opinions about stages and causes of changes, but all agree that human psychological growth occurs over time and that we move through stages in our lives.

In the film *Big*, Tom Hanks play Josh Baskin, a twelve-year-old whose wish to become an adult has magically been fulfilled. The twelve-year-old Josh says, "I want to be big" to a Zoltar fortune-telling machine. His body is transformed into an adult, but he maintains the personality and knowledge of a twelve-year-old. The movie uses comic situations to explore what it means to be an adult. We see the challenges and success of young Josh in the adult world. For a while his innocent youthful point of view rockets him to the top of a toy company. He appreciates more clearly what makes a toy engaging than do the professional toy marketing staff. But ultimately he learns that there is more to being an adult than just being "big."

Growing up is not simply a question of physical stature. Emotional maturity requires an understanding of one's place in the larger world. Newborn infants cannot distinguish where their body ends and the outside world begins. Toddlers imagine that they are the center of the world. The slow process of transformation from child to adult provides ongoing opportunity for growth.

My congregation hosted a dinner in honor of my twenty-five years as its rabbi. One of the speakers described me as being extraordinarily patient. My younger brother Ken laughed. He has a clear memory of my lack of patience. As a child I got angry much more quickly than I do now. I want to be slow to anger. I want to be "big" emotionally.

Years ago Bob Dylan sang, "He not busy being born is busy dying." The process of growth can be seen as a continuing process of birth. In the morning service we praise God as the one who "daily continues to renew the act of creation." We should strive to imitate God and daily renew the act of creating ourselves.

If I reflect over my years as a rabbi, I see progress in my set of skills. My sermons today are certainly more nuanced and sophisticated than those that I wrote during my early years. I have a better understanding of how the decision making process in a congregation should function and how I can play a positive role in that process. But I think that the biggest shift is that I am more patient with other people. I am slower to anger. I can more easily see their point of view. I remain committed to my values and my strongly held beliefs, but I can see the other side of the conversation in a fuller way.

The first step toward growth is to understand in which areas of our lives we need to or want to grow. God urges Jonah to grow. But Jonah remains reluctant. We can do better.

52

Brief Moments

What Makes an Enduring Impact?

And the Eternal said: "You cared about the plant, which you
did not work for, and which you did not grow, which appeared
overnight, and perished overnight." —JONAH 4:10

We learn from our actual teachers. We learn from books we have
read. We learn from the examples of key people in our lives. God
tries to teach an important lesson to Jonah through Jonah's concern
for the *kikayon* plant.

God has to explain to Jonah the meaning of this object lesson
because apparently Jonah cannot figure it out by himself. Ibn Ezra
explains why God uses the plant and the worm to make this point
to Jonah: "The text speaks in this manner so that all who hear it
will know that, does not the Eternal labor on behalf of all his creations?" Speaking to Jonah, God asks, "And this is the reason you
took pity on this thing for which you did nothing? If you feel pity
for this plant, how can I not take pity on all the results of my acts,
all of my creatures?"

Kimchi further unfolds the meaning of God's message to Jonah.
"Even though you did not take pity on the plant except because of
your suffering, the God of Blessing takes pity on Nineveh because
of His glory. For His creatures are His glory. As it is written, 'The
fullness of the earth is His glory' (Isaiah 6:3). And the glory of His
Name is from man. As it is written, 'Whom I created . . . for My
glory' (Isaiah 43:7)." God who created humans cares deeply about
people. God would like Jonah to see that all people have value. But
Jonah seems interested only in himself. Kimchi then turns to the
middle portion of the verse. "When a person labors for something,

he will be sadder when it perishes. And even though the God of Blessing did not actually labor in the forming of His creations, the Torah speaks in the language of people to bring understanding to the listeners."

Malbim adds, "It is the way of the laborer to take pity on the work of his hands and not because the thing itself was valuable and viable." According to Rashi, the tasks included in the term *amalta* are those which Jonah did not perform: "in plowing, planting, and watering."

The Hebrew text describes the *kikayon* as *bin laila*, literally the "son of a night." Ibn Ezra explains, "And understand that it grew up from the beginning of the night until the morning. It lived until the evening, when it fell and dried up completely before the dawn. This is why our text says, 'which appeared overnight and perished overnight.'" Abarbanel adds, "And it wasn't anything about which [you had previously] thought." Before that night in question, Jonah had not even been aware of *kikayon* plants.

We have brief moments in our lives that come in a night and disappear in a night. Sometimes those moments sustain us, just as they did Rick and Ilsa in my favorite movie, *Casablanca*. In the concluding scene Rick says to Ilsa, "We'll always have Paris. We didn't have it, we lost it until you came to Casablanca. We got it back last night. . . . What I've got to do, you can't be any part of. Ilsa, I'm no good at being noble, but it doesn't take much to see that the problems of three little people don't amount to a hill of beans in this crazy world. Someday you'll understand that. . . . Here's looking at you, kid." We viewers know that Rick and Ilsa will always have Paris.

Sometimes brief moments have the power to shape our lives. In June 1969 I visited my parents in the Bay Area. I was at a low point in my life. I was out of school after one year with no plans for my future. One day I drove over the mountains to San Gregorio beach. There I saw a brightly painted old school bus. I chatted with some members of this communal group. I helped them run some errands. They explained that they were on their way to a music festival in Upstate New York. They invited me to come along. I declined the invitation to join the "Hog Farm" on their way to the Woodstock music festival where they gained famed for serving food to 500,000 people. At the time I did not realize that I stood at a fork in the road of my life. I could have dropped out and turned on. It would have made for an exciting summer of adventure. But it certainly would not have led to the path I ended up following.

And brief moments sometimes destroy lives. On June 28, 1914, in Sarajevo, Gavrilo Princip assassinated Archduke Franz Ferdinand of the Austro-Hungarian Empire, sparking World War I. Princip was part of a group of terrorists in Sarajevo that day intent on killing Ferdinand. The events did not unfold as the plotters had planned. A bomb thrown by one of the conspirators blew up one of the cars in the royal procession but not the one carrying Ferdinand and his duchess. In the subsequent confusion, the driver of the car carrying the royal couple made a wrong turn, and the driver stopped the car to turn around. By happenstance, he stopped in front of Princip, who then fired two shots into the car, killing the couple.

This assassination moved the Austro-Hungarian Empire to declare war on Serbia. The Russian Empire, as a result of treaty obligations, Slavic solidarity, and a need to assert itself, declared war on the Austro-Hungarian Empire. The French had treaty obligations to the Russians. The German Empire came in on Austro-Hungary's side and attacked Russia and France. The Germans violated Belgium's neutrality in their attack on France, which moved the English to enter the war on the side of France.

Some people say that World War I was inevitable because of all the military buildup and the web of treaty obligations. The events of history often look inevitable because we already know how events actually played out. Other historians, with whom I agree, argue that this war did not have to take place. Without Princip's assassination of Archduke Franz Ferdinand, World War I might have been avoided. One wrong turn and two bullets led to the death of millions and the destruction of four empires. This brief moment changed the shape of western civilization.

Our entire lives are a brief moment. We do not like to think or talk about the finite nature of our own lives. Most of us easily acknowledge that human history moved along for thousands of years before our birth. But we find it much more difficult to accept that human history will continue to roll on without us after our death. We celebrate our birthdays with cakes, parties, and gifts. But we do not want to think about how our descendants will observe our *yahrzeit* after we have died. Like the *kikayon*, we appear in a night and perish in a night. We can watch what we eat and exercise daily to extend the length of our brief moment. But ultimately it will end. The finite nature of our lives should move us to ask, what have we accomplished? What do we leave behind?

As I mentioned earlier in chapter 17, when my father was dying from pancreatic cancer, I met him in Arizona for Spring Training baseball games. Each afternoon we went to a game. In the morning and evenings we talked. One night over dinner, I apologized to my father for the horrible way I had treated him and my mother when I was nineteen years old. He quickly forgave me. He told me it was not so bad. In truth it was bad, but he was kind and generous to me. My father died twenty-five years ago, but he lives on in my heart. My grandson, his great-grandson, carries his name, as I carry the name of my grandfather. We each came in a night and will perish in a night. While we are here, we touch the lives of many.

We are connected vertically through time to those who came before us and to those who will come after us. The Talmud (Yebamot 97a) tells us that when we repeat the words of our teachers, their lips move in their graves. I feel that way about my teachers, those who taught me face to face and those who I have encountered only through their written words. I know that when I quote Rashi, Ibn Ezra, Kimchi, Abarbanel, and Malbim, I cause their lips to move in their graves.

53

Communities of Meaning

How Can We Create Connections?

And should I not care about Nineveh, that great city, in which there are
more than a hundred and twenty thousand persons who do not yet know
their right hand from their left and many beasts as well! —JONAH 4:11

Jonah acts as if he is all alone. He does not express any concern for
the people of Nineveh. He does not have any traveling companions.
If this story became a Hollywood movie, the producers would probably create a buddy for Jonah. From old westerns to contemporary
police stories, the main character always has a sidekick. The Lone
Ranger had Tonto, Sherlock Holmes had Dr. Watson, Batman had
Robin. But Jonah goes it alone.

In this concluding verse of chapter 4, God continues to explain
forgiveness to Jonah. Abarbanel writes:

[God says to Jonah] And it [Nineveh] is the work of My hand of
which to be proud. And between its size and strength it is not a
kikayon plant. For behold, it has in it many more than 120,000
people. . . . And it is more appropriate to take pity on them. And
you cannot say that you did not pity the *kikayon* plant in its passing when the worm arrived near you to destroy it, for it brought
you shade. And what did I receive from Nineveh? Its great name,
which is like the shade [that the plant brought you]. And if you
say that they practiced idol worship and did not repent from it, I
say they are like human beings who do not speak. For they do not
have Torah and are not commanded by it. And there is a portion
of Hashem in the host of heaven for all nations. And because of
this it is not appropriate to punish them.

The commentators carefully look at the description of the Ninevites in our verse. Ibn Ezra does not take the number 120,000 to
be the population of Nineveh or the number of people who had
repented for their sins but rather the number of people who had not
sinned These two categories of beings, children and animals, could
not be expected to have moral judgment, yet they would have been
destroyed with the rest of the city. Ibn Ezra continues, "For this is
the way we must reason understanding that its destruction would
have been [complete], like the destruction of Sodom. And this matter is known in all the world."

The original Hebrew uses the word *adam* translated here as "people." Kimchi tells us that the number 120,000 should not mistakenly be taken to refer to the number of men in Nineveh. It includes
"men and women." Rashi explains that the phrase "who do not yet
know their right hand from their left" refers to children who are too
young to have yet learned this distinction. They would have been
killed in the destruction of Nineveh, and the word *beasts* refers to
"grown adults whose thinking is like that of animals who do not
know who created them."

Kimchi agrees with Rashi. "They are children who do not know
the difference between their right and their left. And they have no
sin and deserve no punishment except on account of their parents.
And because the parents repented, the children are without punishment." But Kimchi disagrees with Rashi concerning the meaning of
the phrase "and many beasts." He understands it to be literally referring to animals. "And so the many animals they had in the city. And
the animal deserved no punishment and all of these living creatures
deserve [God's] concern and protection and even more so because
of their number."

Abarbanel presents a different way of reading the phrase "who do
not yet know their right hand from their left." He explains:

And God does not say this in reference to infants as other inter-
preters [Rashi and Kimchi] have said. For in this condemned city

the infants were judged for the sins of their parents, for they are like limbs of the adults, and their fate [is the fate of the adults of the city]. But He says this about the population of Nineveh in general. For in the city there are more than 120,000 people without [the benefit of the teachings of the] Torah. So in the matter of idol worship, they do not know their right from their left.

Malbim suggests that the phrase "who do not yet know their right hand from their left" describes the Ninevites' inability to distinguish between Israelite religion and their own pagan practices:

For they do not have the knowledge to distinguish between the worship of special God represented by the right hand. As is written, "Yet I was always with You, / You held my right hand" (Psalms 73:23). And the worship of the left is worship of nature and array [of heavenly bodies] which are connected to the left side. And they should not be punished because of their lack of knowledge.

And from this we receive an answer also concerning the punishment of Israel. For they already learned the difference between right and left. For they received the [Torah containing the] knowledge of God and the true faith. And they are appropriately punished for any idolatrous worship they perform. And the people of Nineveh are not punished for this. [God explains to Jonah that the Ninevites deserve mercy because they are not an advanced society.]

While the commentators differ in how they assign specific meaning to the metaphors used to describe the Ninevites, they all agree that God is telling Jonah that the Ninevites need to be taken seriously as human beings. They have intrinsic value simply because they *are* people. The original Hebrew uses singular forms, *"lo yada bein-y'mino lismolo,"* who does not know his right hand from his left, to refer to each of the Ninevites, emphasizing their individual worth.

The prophet Malachi proclaims, "Do we not all have one Father? Did not one God create us?" (Malachi 2:10)

While we moderns do not take the story of the creation of the first man and women in Genesis literally, we should firmly hold to its metaphoric meaning—our common ancestry. We should treat other people as members of our family. We are connected horizontally through space to those in whose midst we live. We need community. We need communities of meaning. Utopian communes have drawn participants because of the human support they promise. Over the centuries people have sought out isolated religious orders. We do not need to retreat from the world to find a meaningful community. A healthy congregation should be such a place. A congregation should be a place where everybody knows and cares about you.

The book of Jonah ends abruptly without telling us Jonah's response to God's lesson. Does Jonah learn? The sailors learned; they recognized the Eternal as the ruler of the universe. They made vows and sacrifices. The people of Nineveh learned; they repented for their sins and turned to God. Does Jonah learn? Is Jonah going to walk with God? By not answering this question, the author allows us to insert ourselves into the story at the end. Did we learn? Are we going to follow the examples of the sailors and the Ninevites by turning to God? Will we see the importance of the other people in our lives? Or will we remain self-absorbed like Jonah?

Jonah acts as if he is the only one who counts. The meaning in our lives grows from realizing that we are not alone. It comes not from examining ourselves in isolation but rather by knowing that we are connected vertically through time to those who came before us and to those who will come after us, and horizontally through space to those in whose midst we live. And we are connected beyond the limits of time and space to the Eternal. The word of God "is not too baffling for you, nor is it beyond reach. It is not in heaven, that you should say, 'Who will go up to heaven for us to get it for us and impart it to us, that we may observe it?' Nor is it beyond the sea, that you should say, 'Who will cross the sea for us to get it for us and impart it to us, that we may observe it?' No, the thing is very close to you, in your mouth and in your heart, to observe it" (Deuteronomy 30:11–14).

OTHER WORKS BY STEVEN BOB

Go to Nineveh (Pickwick Press, 2013)

The Madrichim Manual, with Lisa Bob Howard (Behrman House, 2006)

"Yom HaShoah for Christians and Jews," in *Holocaust and Church Struggle*, edited by Hubert G. Locke and Marcia Sachs Littell (University Press of America, 1996)

Azari's
Alan

CPSIA information can be obtained
at www.ICGtesting.com
Printed in the USA
LVOW12s1049010416
481697LV00003B/3/P

9 780827 612204